ASCENTS AND DESCENTS

ASCENTS AND DESCENTS

An alpinist's memoir

PETER ALLISON

bâton wicks

Bâton Wicks, Sheffield
www.v-publishing.co.uk/batonwicks

ASCENTS AND DESCENTS

PETER ALLISON

First published in 2019 by Bâton Wicks, an imprint of Vertebrate Publishing.

Vertebrate Publishing
Omega Court, 352 Cemetery Road, Sheffield S11 8FT United Kingdom.
www.v-publishing.co.uk

This book is a work of non-fiction based on the life of Peter Allison. The author has stated
to the publishers that, except in such minor respects not affecting the substantial accuracy
of the work, the contents of the book are true.

A CIP catalogue record for this book is available from the British Library.

ISBN 978-1-898573-84-5 (Paperback)

10 9 8 7 6 5 4 3 2 1

Design and production by Vertebrate Publishing.
www.v-publishing.co.uk

Bâton Wicks and Vertebrate Publishing are committed to printing on paper from sustainable sources.

MIX
Paper from
responsible sources
FSC® C013056

Printed and bound in UK by T.J. International Ltd, Padstow, Cornwall.

CONTENTS

Foreword by David Hopkins vii
Introduction xv

Chapter 1 **The Early Years** 1
Chapter 2 **Ice Climbing Development** 13
Chapter 3 **Motorcars** 23
Chapter 4 **Rock** 31
Chapter 5 **The Eiger Days** 41
Chapter 6 **Soloing** 49
Chapter 7 **Skiing** 57
Chapter 8 **Business** 63
Chapter 9 **Guiding** 75
Chapter 10 **Old Friends** 101
Chapter 11 **Old Age** 111
Chapter 12 **The Final Chapter: 'The Big C'** 121

About the Author 125

David Hopkins (left) and Peter (centre). © David Hopkins

FOREWORD BY DAVID HOPKINS

It was on Tuesday 3 January 2017 that I last climbed with Peter Allison. We went up to the Crèmerie in Argentière for a 'potter about'. Not only was the ice pretty sketchy but we also had to be alert to the number of novices scratching, scrambling and eventually falling off all around us. Having escaped the crowds, we quickly established ourselves at the belay below the steepening. As was customary, Peter in his inimitable way 'volunteered' to lead the crux pitch! That, however, did give me a particularly advantageous position from which to observe him exercise his craft. I have always been impressed with Peter's technical ability, poise and efficiency while climbing, and that day looking across at him I understood why. The ice was steep, brittle and gnarly, yet Peter's footwork, centre of gravity and precision were exemplary. He just 'smoothed' up the pitch. Thinking of that now, it is the control of and total oneness with his environment that I see; simultaneously I recall the words of Gerard Manley Hopkins – 'the achieve of, the mastery of the thing!'

The next Monday, Peter went powder skiing on the Grands Montets with a number of close friends and came home ecstatic and energised. The following Wednesday, he met with Patrick Bettin, our GP in Argentière – a consultation that began a journey that had its culmination in his death on Monday 2 October 2017. During the intervening nine months Peter bore his illness with the bravery, stoicism and optimism that has characterised all his being. It was yet another example that Peter gave us of how to live the good life, while obstinately and passionately still 'raging against the dying of the light.'

To many of us Peter defined himself as a climber, alpinist and guide. He took much pleasure in creating that persona and lifestyle, particularly following his 'retirement' in early middle age. Peter could be at times a private person despite the social and gregarious personality that many saw on and off the hill. It should therefore come as little surprise that Peter put significant effort over the past few years into writing an autobiographical memoir. He mentioned it to me *en passant* a couple of years ago and I offered to read it and help find a publisher. At that point Peter became characteristically coy and self-deprecating – 'it is only a few recollections, just some jottings – but you know that I have been around a long time and some people may find what I have to say helpful … '

Ten days before his passing, when he was in St David's Hospice in Llandudno, North Wales, Peter with his wife Sylvie began to discuss his will, the funeral service and the spreading of his ashes, and then mentioned his memoirs again. He told Sylvie where they were, and later we found 250 handwritten pages carefully edited into a book of twelve chapters, replete with photographs and entitled *Ascents and Descents – the ups and downs of sixty-six years of climbing and ski-mountaineering*. We later found the final chapter among his papers in the hospice. During that conversation, Peter asked me to read the manuscript with a view to guiding it towards publication. It was a request that has been an honour and a real pleasure to respond to.

Peter introduced his memoir as follows:

> *There are probably lots of folk who have rock climbed for fifty years or so, and no doubt there are many mature people who have skied the pistes for maybe sixty years, but there cannot be many who have been rock climbers, ice climbers, alpinists, mountaineers, solo climbers, ski-mountaineers and steep skiers for as long as sixty-five years, who started rock climbing in 1951 with hemp rope and socks over plimsolls, and who keep on doing it all at seventy-five years old.*
>
> *There cannot be many who have soloed hard climbs and skied fifty-degree alpine couloirs that they chopped footsteps up, with one straight wooden ice axe, to climb as a youth, almost sixty years earlier.*
>
> *And if there are it's unlikely that they've had a 'full-on' business career as well, or that they then spent many years as a professional mountain guide taking clients for adventures in the mountains all around the world.*

In introducing Peter's memoir let me use some of his own words, in chronicling his achievements as a rock climber, alpinist, extreme skier and guide.

Rock climber – Peter evolved as a rock climber like most of us 'oldies', who, without the benefit of climbing walls, began with climbing trees and scrambling in local woods and quarries. His first real graded route was on Crag Lough on Hadrian's Wall when he was only ten years old. Then as a young teenager he increasingly found his way out and about by hitch-hiking and riding his bike on to the gritstone edges and then on to the Lakes and North Wales. Despite using the most rudimentary gear, from the beginning Peter was technically excellent. His footwork was always precise and he rapidly progressed to repeating the hardest of routes from the Brown era and was enthusiastically involved in the early exploration of Gogarth. Peter could also be very bold and he soon accumulated a collection of impressive solo ascents, including probably the first – or at least very early – solos of both *Vector* and *Cenotaph Corner*.

> *After a fast drive over, I got out in the pass fairly buzzing. I felt good and confident so [I scrambled up and then] set off soloing up Cenotaph Corner. At the niche there was still an in-situ peg and I put a finger through it, not for aid or anything, but just to shake out a bit and stop and think. But then, within seconds I thought, 'Don't think. That leads to loss of concentration. Just get on with it. Don't even think about thinking, for goodness sake.' I just bridged up a bit, laid away on the finger jam to reach the good handholds past the crux, and cruised over the top. I still felt very calm while scrambling down the descent gully and then allowed myself to consider that more soling was possible, if you just stay calm and composed.*

Alpinist – Like many of his generation Peter followed the traditional apprenticeship of an aspiring mountaineer: local crags, gritstone, the Lakes and Wales, then Scotland and eventually the Alps. However, unlike many of his generation, Peter progressed through this induction very rapidly. His first alpine season was in 1957 in the Austrian Alps and he was soon ticking off an impressive series of north faces and grandes courses. Climbing with his elder brother, they searched out north faces that had not had a British ascent. In doing this, Peter claims that they discovered 'simul-climbing' – whether this was more to do with sibling rivalry or lack of gear, I will let you decide! Among these early ascents were the north faces of the Lyskamm, Leschaux and the Aiguille de Triolet, *Route Major*, the *Walker Spur* and the *Frendo Spur*. Perhaps the most impressive of this series of ascents was Peter's solo of the North Face of the Matterhorn; but the one of which he was most proud was his ascent with Smiler Cuthbertson of the North Face of the Eiger. The following description of an aspect of that ascent gives a clear picture of Peter's intuition and decision-making while attempting challenging ascents, and illustrates well why he was such a safe climber.

There is nowhere where timing is more important than on the second and third ice fields on the Eiger North Wall. By late morning the sun loosens all those rocks in the ice near the summit and the bombardment of stonefall starts. So if you sleep at the Swallows' Nest Bivouac, you'll be too late at the dangerous sections. Okay, the Swallows' Nest is comfortable and safe, but it is too low down. God has put it in the wrong place. As it was, with my plan we could only get short 'power naps' on our tiny ledge, but by dawn we were up our abseil rope and after several hours of motoring we were up to the Flat Iron section and then the so-called Death Bivouac. By midday we were across the dangerous last ice field, which is crucial, and safely on to the Ramp. I had always wanted to climb it when frozen up in icy conditions with a minimum of stonefall, even though it meant climbing every single pitch in crampons.

Extreme skier – Like many of his generation Peter came to skiing late. His first attempt was as an 'inebriated student in a field one winter, wearing wellington boots and using old wooden skis off somebody's ornament wall. It did not go well!' Later, the desire to climb north faces in winter meant that he had to learn how to ski, and that led Peter into ski-mountaineering – an aspect of the discipline on which he would become an expert. As with so many other things, when Peter put his considerable intelligence, passion and athletic ability into an endeavour, not only did he succeed, but he also became a master. From those early days Peter's development as a skier took him on and then off the piste, through deep powder, and latterly to extreme skiing. He was justly proud of his descent in 2016 of the Chevalier Couloir.

During the winter of 2016, I got a bit carried away one day. I was climbing up the north side of the Petite Aiguille Verte, which is a little peak below the main Aiguille Verte and above the Grands Montets ski lift system. I was skinning up the lower slopes when two young Swedish lads came tearing up behind me, and went up to the summit snow ridge, which is like a half moon. They were going to ski the Chevalier Couloir. They must have had the illusion that I was thirty years younger than I am because they kept on asking me to join them.

Anselme Baud's guidebook says that the couloir is 'Sustained and the top section can be more than fifty-five degrees – and you use a rope to start.' So we chopped down the big cornice and looked down, and I thought it looked absolutely outrageous! I assumed these guys would drop a rope down and abseil into it, but it turned out that they were modern superstars who had skied the north face of the Aiguille du Midi. So these two guys clipped into their skis and just sort of dropped in. I nearly had a fit. Then they skied down, passing each other and making video films.

Fifty-five-degree snow through rocks is way too exciting for me on skis nowadays. In fact, it always was! So I cramponed down for a bit with two ice axes until it relented to an old man's angle. Then I chopped out a ledge in the snow to get my crampons off and skis on, and then skied it from there. Even then, there was a triple bergschrund to cross at the bottom and that needed some very precise turns to negotiate, and a bit of a jump. Then it was just 2,100 metres more vertical down the glacier and pistes to the valley, relief and a brew.

Peter reflected on the descent:

Overcommitment when you're young comes from boldness and leads to innovation, development, exploration, expansion and progress. Overcommitment when you're really old comes from stupidity. I think it's time to back off a bit now; I'm seventy-five years old, for goodness sake!

Guide – Peter took much pride and pleasure in his third profession, a mountain guide, which he embarked on as he was coming up to the age of fifty. As a teenager climbing in the Lake District he came across stories of Millican Dalton, the self-styled 'Professor of Adventure' who lived in that large cave in Borrowdale. He saw Millican's advertisement, 'Professor of Adventure, near misses almost guaranteed'. Peter wryly commented that claiming 'near misses definitely avoided' would have brought in more custom! Peter saw himself following Millican Dalton's tradition and example.

His motivation for becoming a guide was that he 'fancied putting something back into the climbing world, maybe helping people to fulfil their mountaineering ambitions and keeping them safe in what we all know to be a risky environment.' His many clients fulsomely attest to how, as a guide, Peter was caring, competent and safe.

Peter himself wrote that:

> *A professional guide has to be continuously thinking one step ahead, about what possibly could go wrong, and be ready to improvise and deal with every eventuality.*

Many of us have reason to be grateful to Peter, not just for his safety consciousness, problem solving and care, but also for opening up vistas and experiences that we could have only dreamt about. Those of us who are guides respected him as a consummate professional and a real 'brother in arms'.

In reflecting on his life in the mountains Peter wrote:

> *It's not bad for some skinny kid who had tied a bowline around his waist on a single bit of damp rope, back in about 1951, and climbed in tatty Woolworths gym shoes, sometimes with socks over the top when it was wet.*

But those of us who were privileged to know him, also knew that Peter was much more than just a climber, alpinist and guide. He was a challenging, energising, thoughtful and deeply loyal friend to many, both on and off the hill. Peter also took much pleasure in being a fine father to Martin, Simon and Kate and a much-loved Papa to Callum, Ruby, Archie and Oliver. He was married to Jancis, the mother of Martin and Simon, and then to Sylvie, the mother of Kate who became his stepdaughter.

It was Sylvie who provided Peter with the shelter conditions to both achieve some peace with himself and fulfil his potential as the complete mountaineer. In reflecting on their relationship, Peter wrote:

> *There are very few other people in the whole world that are the right partner for any one person; with the right character, personality, interests, background, attitudes, looks, etc. If you are lucky enough to find that person, then you are indeed very lucky: a good soulmate is for life.*

While rereading these pages prior to publication, I found myself almost continuously smiling and occasionally laughing out loud at Peter's wry humour, acute observations and at times affected self-deprecation. Peter's own voice came so strongly off the page that it was as if we were having a conversation in their living room in Argentière, with that glorious view over Mont Blanc in the background.

But on reflection, I also began to realise that this was something more than just old friends exchanging travellers' tales or the reliving of past adventures. As a rock climber and alpinist Peter lived through some of the most formative times in British mountaineering. As will be seen on the pages that follow, being so active in the 1960s and 1970s, Peter experienced and helped shape the next phase of development in UK climbing. He chronicles authentically the 'post-Brown' era both on British rock and in the Alps, so giving personal insights into how techniques and equipment evolved to generate even higher standards of achievement.

So, this memoir is not just a series of personal reminiscences, it is also a piece of lived mountaineering history that illustrates how British climbing began to mature, and captures the spirit of that age. It is here in the deft interweaving of the personal and the historical that the power and value of Peter's memoir lies.

David Hopkins

Peter on ascent of the North Face of the Col du Plan with David Hopkins
and Peter Williams, 2002. © Peter Allison Collection

INTRODUCTION

I've been climbing now for sixty-five years.

I first started rock climbing in about 1951 using a hemp rope and plimsolls. Woolworths plimsolls were very cheap and the rubber soles were quite good. But then they started to make the soles out of plastic, which was much cheaper, but they were slippy, so we used to pull wool socks over the top of them to get more friction.

I started ice climbing in the mid-1950s in the Lake District, cutting steps with a single, straight wooden ice axe up snow slopes and gentle ice pitches.

My first trip to the European Alps was in 1957 as a schoolboy, on a bus with wooden seats; my first attempts at skiing were with long wooden planks with rusty cable bindings, strapped on to wellington boots – for a laugh. All these years later, in 2016, I'm still trying to do it all, albeit with modern gear and a sort of rough approximation of modern techniques.

I've considered if there are many other folks who have climbed for as long as sixty-five years, with long experience of cragging, alpinism, mountaineering, soloing routes close to their limits and professional guiding in the mountains around the world. I have climbing friends older than me who maybe started about 1948 or so, but most stopped a while back. There are others who started much later, in the 1960s, and so they missed out on the pleasures of rock climbing and snow and ice climbing using our delightful early equipment. Then there are lots of young hotshots, of course, who have climbed much harder than me, but not many who have had proper jobs and careers as well – and not many of those have skied on the modern steep stuff.

So there are few who have undergone the long transition from using simple old-fashioned equipment and techniques to employing modern high-tech gear and skills applicable to the different climbing and skiing sports of today. But there are not many who have soloed big routes, skied steeps and guided professionally as well. Nowadays, we're skiing fifty-degree faces that in the 1950s we'd have struggled to cut steps up to climb.

So now, after suggestions from various friends and guiding colleagues who have written books themselves, I've considered that some ancient old codger like me should try and make a rough record of the changes, transitions and developments that have taken place in equipment and techniques during these last sixty-five years, which have included the so-called 'Golden Age' of mountain sports. I've never written anything myself before and I've never kept a diary; digging through these memories has been fascinating for me in trying to recall lots of stuff, in roughly the correct order.

Memories are never quite accurate. We remember good bits and maybe we're programmed to forget the bad bits so that we can cope with life. Witnesses will always recall the same events in completely different ways. That has happened to me a lot.

Although this story is largely about climbing and ski-mountaineering, it's more a ramble through my life, with a fair bit of 'social history' thrown in, and lots of references to changing styles of ice climbing equipment and techniques. There's a lot about skiing, including some about the steeper stuff. There's a bit about motorcars, business things and a past career. Then there is a big chunk about professional mountain guiding. I've included a little of my memories of when I was soloing silly things, and there's lots of stuff about avalanches, the mountain environment and safety issues, and about how to survive it all and – hopefully – stay alive.

There are lots of the 'ups': the climbing 'ups', the 'ups' of the harder climbs, and the Alpine north faces. And there are some of the 'downs': the skiing 'downs' and the down 'downs' – like getting roasted in a thousand-gallon diesel-oil fire, the long years of recovery from a broken pelvis, and a detached retina eye operation.

I've included some of my experiences of wildlife in the mountains and I couldn't help but discuss so many of my good friends who, over the years, have simply not survived. The mountains of the world are wonderful places, but we have to respect their power.

I am not going to mention many specific names, partly because of old-age memory problems and partly because I don't want to be sued. So if anyone recognises bits about themselves that sound good, then thank you for the great adventures. If you recognise yourself in libellous bits, then I deny everything. I wasn't there; it was someone else.

Peter on *Chequers Buttress*, Froggatt Edge. © Peter Allison Collection

Chapter 1
THE EARLY YEARS

I was born fairly early on in the war years, in north-east England. My father was away shooting down Messerschmitts or something that was trying to bomb the docks. In fact, it took me a long time to deduce that he had probably been given a rollicking for letting the diesel engine generators for the search lights freeze up one winter, because he was always obsessed with antifreeze in engines.

I reckon the German pilots should have gone to Specsavers, because quite a few of their bombs seemed to fall pretty randomly.

We had an air raid shelter. It was called the kitchen table. My mother and I hid under said kitchen table with a big thick 'proddy' mat over our heads when the bombs were dropping. A proddy mat was a thick homemade rug, made by prodding strips of scrap cloth through the weave of a hessian backing. Later on, I made one with a picture of a Spitfire on it.

I didn't meet my father until I was about seven, when he came back from the army. He probably wondered who I was, and I certainly thought 'Who on earth are you?' I was the middle of three boys. Eldest was close to Father and youngest was close to Mother. I don't remember my father ever calling me by my right name. I think it was a case of good, old-fashioned, healthy neglect.

Fortunately, I had an older and eccentric Uncle Archie who wore plus fours and spots. Family rumour was that he had joined the Royal Flying Corps under age sixteen. He used to tell tales that in the First World War he flew canvas biplanes – Sopwith Camels, I suppose – over the German trenches to take photographs. Sadly, the German pilots were not honourable gentlemen and fired pistols at them from their Junkers. He told me that the British then took bits of fishing nets, with house bricks tied to each corner, up with them and dropped them on the German propellers. That wouldn't do them a lot of good. You couldn't make that up, so I guess it must have been true. I certainly wore his fur and leather flying helmet with ear flaps much later on, during a long spell of driving only open-top, old cars.

I remember swimming in the North Sea off the Northumberland coast as a youngster because my Auntie Nellie, who eventually reached ninety-nine-and-a-half years old, lived there. Her husband had been killed in a coal mining explosion in the 1920s, and she'd been a widow for many years. The North Sea was seriously cold and the wind blew straight across from the urinals. I suppose the adults actually meant the Urals, but I'm still not entirely sure.

When I was about seven years old, we had the only family holiday that I remember, and we went to Whitby. In those days, you could still pick up pieces of jet on the shingle beach. Anyway, there were rowing boats for hire that weren't allowed out of the harbour. But there was a bell-buoy exactly one mile beyond the pier, so Uncle Archie rowed us both out and around this bell-buoy and we went fishing for cod and whiting with a piece of string and a bent pin somewhere in the middle of the North Sea. We didn't catch anything, of course, but I remember being 'gripped' (that's mountaineering speak for terrified).

But that wasn't my first epic in life. For some daft reason my mother sent me to infant school about five miles from home, instead of to a local one. I had to catch the bus, on my own, from five years old. One day, the bus came around the corner and stopped and I grabbed the vertical handle to climb up the steps, but the door didn't open, and the driver pulled away. I was left hanging from the handle with my legs trailing along the tarmac and unable to let go because I'd have gone under the back wheels. Eventually some old biddy screamed, and the driver stopped. I was short of a fair bit of skin off my legs.

My first climbing incident was at about six years old in the local recreation park, or 'down the rec.' There were children's swings and slides and a thing we called the 'shuggy boat' which was a circular wooden seat suspended from a pyramid of bars and supported on a solid steel cone at the top of a central pole. The whole thing went up and down as we pushed it round and round. An older kid said there was a bird's nest in the cone at the top, and so stupid me, like the original failed hero, climbed up the bars to the top and stuck my hand into the cone, just as the other part crashed down on to it. I've still got the scars from the splits up the sides of my fingers and thumb.

In the 1940s coal, milk and bread were delivered in the north-east by horse and cart. The horses obviously had horseshoes, but in winter the shoes had extra studs in them to grip the icy roads. These studs were sort of star-shaped and must have been difficult to make, but they kept coming out of the shoes. As kids we collected these studs in the gutters and returned them to the local blacksmith who, in return, gave us iron runners that we fitted to homemade wooden sledges.

We had this quite famous sledging track that came about half a mile down the local escarpment. It started off down a farm track and then went through lots of gorse bushes before looping under a barbed wire fence, around the edge of an old sandstone quarry, down another icy cart track, through a farm gate that we left open and finally out on to a frozen pond. We went head first and steering was a very sophisticated affair: you just trailed your left or right welly.

One cold snowy winter in the late 1940s, the local baker's apprentice lad missed a turn in the gorse bushes, went through the barbed wire fence over into the quarry and was killed. The council tried to shut it down and the farmer built fences across it. Kids had come from miles around to try our sledging track. The Cresta Run had nothing on our nursery playground.

One childish ambition of mine was, for some silly reason, to climb my mother's seven-foot clothes post in the garden – maybe even to stand on the top. It was stupidly impossible of course, but in 1947 there was about five feet of snow in north-eastern gardens, with great big drifts of windblown snow, so there were only a couple of feet of this post showing above the snow. In the end, realising that ambition was an absolute doddle. Clearly it was just a question of being patient and then snatching the ideal conditions for such a stunt. So I learnt early on that timing is absolutely everything in life. For example, nowadays it's easy to find bad snow to ski. The clever bit is finding good snow, when everything else is bad. And for the seasonal mountain routes you've got to wait and snatch things when conditions are just right. A good lesson learnt.

My next outdoor adventure was a rafting one. At about nine years old, we rolled some empty oil barrels from a local garage down to the River Wear. We tied some branches together with string that we'd found and made a raft of sorts. But in the middle of the river, which seemed to be in spate, we realised that one barrel had a hole in it and our raft became a bit lop-sided with a list to starboard in the rapids. When a huge bridge abutment loomed across our path we were shipwrecked and had a soggy six-mile walk home. A mountaineering pal nowadays defines a proper 'adventure' as something where you might not actually come back home. Our nautical rafting adventure on the Wear wasn't quite in that category, but it was still pretty gripping at the age of nine.

My first long trek was also at nine, with older relations. We walked up the River Tees from Low Falls to the spectacular High Force Falls, which was said to be the highest waterfall in England, and which I climbed up solo with crampons and ice axes when it froze in the winter of 1977. Then we carried on above the waterfalls of Cauldron Spout to where the dam and reservoir are now. At nine years old I was knackered.

My first mountain adventure was at ten years old, and again it was with my uncles and Auntie Mabel. We walked from the River Tees up Maize Beck right over the Pennines and down the classic High Cup Nick, which is the best U-shaped glaciated valley in Britain, and then finally up Dufton Pike, for a total of about twenty-one miles. Dufton Pike is hardly a mountain, but it's a proper summit when you're only ten. Again, I was clapped out.

This was also the age I graduated from climbing trees to scrambling up boulder problems and cracks and corners in an old sandstone quarry just a mile or so from our house. I was desperate for a bike and eventually my father got me a third-hand, wartime contraption made from cast iron. The pedals would turn the chain and the back sprocket, but that didn't turn the back wheel, so I took the wheel off. As a budding rocket-scientist I hit the sprocket with a brick and that riveted something over so that the sprocket actually turned the back wheel. Unfortunately, the wheel wouldn't then freewheel, but at least it would drive, leaving me with a fixed-gear bike, just like the bone-shakers of the 1850s. With a fixed-gear bike the pedals keep turning, so you can slow down by resisting the pedals. Brakes are then not really necessary. Wartime bike brakes were operated by heavy rods, rather than cables, so they were just excess weight. I streamlined my machine by throwing them away. I bodged some fancy drop handlebars and suddenly I had transport. I was then able to spend summer holidays at my grandmother's little farm helping my uncle to bring in the hay using a chain-sweep behind a big cart horse. My uncle got an old 1920s Fordson Major tractor instead, which I learnt to drive and repair. Even James Herriot couldn't have fixed his big carthorse, but the old tractor was easy. It didn't have a bad temper for me to deal with.

My first proper graded rock climb, as in the climbing guidebooks, was at

Crag Lough on Hadrian's Wall in Northumberland when I was about ten years old. It was the school holidays and I was walking with an auntie and uncle. Some lads from Newcastle were failing to get up *West Chimney*. I must have been a bit nosy and quite interested watching them, and so they must have thought I was daft enough to try. They tied me on to their hemp rope and I somehow managed to lead it. I think it's graded 'very difficult', but that's very easy in modern terms. As I said, this was with a hemp rope. All that nonsense about mother's old clothes line is rubbish. Wartime clothes lines weren't even strong enough to make a swing on a tree. Their breaking strain was about two shirts and three pairs of socks and certainly didn't include the weight of a skinny little lad wearing them.

By thirteen I was cycling across the Pennines to the Lake District and sleeping in barns in Borrowdale. At fourteen I did *Kern Knotts Crack* on Great Gable. At fifteen I led *Thirlmere Eliminate* on Castle Rock in a pair of Woolworths plimsolls, which Don Whillans had just done. There was a piton at the bulge then, which I'm sure I must have pulled on, because I did it again fifty-odd years later and there was no peg. I confess to having found it quite hard the second time, though in my defence, being well into my sixties, I was starting to suffer from skiers' knees.

I suppose I didn't have much imagination as a youth and never thought about falling off and going for big 'purlers', but even naïve young me realised that belay anchors and waist belays weren't much good in those days. Instead, I remember making big figure-of-eight knots in hemp slings and jamming them into cracks, as anchors for belaying to.

It used to take me a day and a half to cycle to the Lake District over the Pennines against the westerly head winds, sleeping overnight in the same phone box. I could however, always come back in about four hours with a big coat on to catch the following wind, just like a big spinnaker sail.

In the old days, there had been coach houses at five-mile intervals on this road, for changing horses. Many years later one of them had become a cafe with new owners, a young couple from London. I asked them how they liked living up on the moors and hills. 'Great,' they said, 'but what are the twelve-foot-high red and white poles at the sides of the roads for?' In 1947, I remember three metres of snow in Teesdale, so I told them to wait for the winter and then they'd find out.

As a teenager, I used to hitch-hike up to the summit of the moors in winter and get out when a car got stuck in the snow. Then I'd walk a few miles over the top, and hitch a lift back down the other side into Cumbria from a driver who'd driven up the west side and got stuck in the snow there. Later on, bivouacs in storms on Alpine north faces were a bit of a doddle after school-boy winter epics in the northern Pennines. Until Beeching closed the little railways, there had been a train over the Pennines to the Lakes, and I used it once when I had a few shillings and stayed in a barn in Borrowdale. I met a lad who was a mad-keen walker and so we got up early and jogged around the Lakeland 3,000ers: Scafell, Scafell Pike over to Helvellyn, and then up to Skiddaw. We got back down to a pub in Keswick, wacked out again, but the barman wouldn't serve me a drink, because I was only fifteen.

About that time, there was an incident at school. I was quite keen on wild flowers, because of cycling through remote woods and places, and had a col-lection of about 500. As a result, I was a mate of the biology master who gave me the charming summer holiday job of cycling into the school and feeding his cages of locusts. I collected freshly cut grass from our rugby field and stuffed it into the cage doors. One day I wasn't quick enough. As I opened one door, a big aggressive beast leapt out and as I tried to grab it another one snuck out too. By the time I'd thrown a cloth over it and got yet another one back inside, there were half a dozen of the horrible things all over the labora-tory. All I could do was slam the lab door and clear off. Needless to say, I wasn't too keen on returning the next day. I crept back in and where there had been five-metre-high green curtains up against all the windows, now there were just shredded strips of remnants and lots of big fat ugly creatures with daft grins, sat all over the benches. Unsurprisingly, I was no longer pals with the biology master.

There was another, more final, incident at school. It was the last day and we'd bought some iodine from a chemist's shop, so in the chemistry lab we made a schoolboy version of TNT, but a bit less aggressive. When we spread a few crystals on the corridor floors and a bit on the headmaster's door handle there were little bangs everywhere. The fifth and sixth formers were all called into assembly and being honest sort of lads we owned up and were asked to go home early. Sort of expelled, I suppose.

I'd discovered climbing on gritstone – God's own rock – in Yorkshire, Derbyshire and later on eventually in Staffordshire. The friction is fantastic, and the gritstone edges are designed and built by a pretty good architect and bricklayer, just perfect for rock climbers. By the late 1950s, we were climbing the cracks and slabs of grit and sometimes soloing the easy things.

One day at Black Rocks near Matlock, I met these two guys who had a string of big, heavy, ex-war-department, steel karabiners. They turned out to be Pete Biven and Trevor Peck, who were heroes of the previous climbing generation. We explored High Tor, cutting out a few points of aid on the existing classics, and linking up a new girdle traverse. The gamekeeper caught us at the top and gave us a rollicking, claiming that he'd 'soloed up there with a shotgun and two rabbits.' But I thought that was highly unlikely because the route we finished up is still graded about E2.

In 1957 I first went to the European Alps, all the way to Austria in a bus with desperate wooden seats. I went with a boy from school; we walked up one easy hill fine, then scrambled up another one a bit steeper. He got a bit gripped and went back down, but I went and scrambled up another one, the 'Pic d'Insignificance' or something. However, that was steeper still and so I got gripped as well. But it was quite rocky at the top and it felt great. A challenge that he hadn't been able to do. An adventure and a buzz. And then extremely careful concentration to get back down safely.

It gave me a strong feeling that there was a whole new world out there, full of big mountains and exciting, top-quality routes to be climbed. It was the start of a big new adventure and, as the future panned out, since that first 1957 Austrian bus trip I've only missed one summer alpine trip. This was when I failed my university second year exams and had three summer jobs to finance my resit year.

One summer, a school pal and I hitched from the north-east of England to Cornwall, about 500 miles. We were fifteen years old and camped in a field next to the bungalow of two old ladies. They fed us for several weeks with their home-grown fresh tomatoes, and we went surfing and climbing on the Cornish sea cliffs. Remarkably, we returned home in just two lifts. One took us all the way to London's North Circular and then we secured one lift from there all the way up to Durham with a film actor in a big flash motor.

On another school holiday, a friend's family took me to North Wales where I wandered around the cliffs of Llanberis Pass for the first time. I met a lad from London who had a rope and I led a climb on Clogwyn y Grochan in the shoes that I happened to be wearing. It turned out to be called *Karwendel Wall*. The lad was Tim Lewis, and I know this for certain because he was with another lad who took photos, and he turned out to be climbing photographer Ken Wilson. We found the photos many, many years later when we were rummaging through Ken's drawers of old pictures at his home in London. At the time, we thought that we'd done *Kaisergebirge Wall*, but this photograph proved otherwise.

Much later on, talking to Hugh Banner in the pub before his motorbike accident, he said that in 1958 on his first ascent, he thought somebody had been up *Karwendel Wall* previously. This was because there's a long reach for a good handhold, and someone had pulled off some loose rock to make the good hold; Ken had the evidence in black and white.

Also in the mid-1950s, I had been in the Lake District one winter weekend when someone had fallen from Great End Buttress and slid a long way down the snow slopes covering the scene. After helping with the rescue, I later found an old wooden Austrian ice axe, and I then used that with some simple crampons that had been abandoned in a Fell and Rock hut. They were broken but I managed to bodge them up with some wire, and then I was able to follow one of the Lakeland old masters, climbing up frozen streambeds and little frozen waterfalls, working out how to cut steps in steeper snow slopes and bits of ice. Within a couple of winters, I got quite keen and then one winter day I soloed all the classic gullies on Great End Buttress in just a few hours, when they were in a fairly easy condition. I felt ready for Scotland.

I scrounged a lift up to Ben Nevis and went up to the Charles Inglis Clark (CIC) mountain hut that was full of tough and famous Glaswegian mountaineers. They said 'Ye cannae come in here, wee laddie. It's private', and kicked us out. So I experienced my first winter bivouac out in the snow with very little gear. However, we still managed to chop steps up a couple of their easier Scottish classics.

One very cold winter in about 1960, two of the local climbing lads died while sleeping in their van beside Derwent Water, near Keswick. They had brewed up in the van, which melted the snow on the roof, and meltwater filled around the door and window seal, which then froze up in the night. They died of asphyxiation. The police found them the next day and warned us all about cooking and sleeping in vans – just the same as snow holes really.

About the same time in one of those brutal winters, we did an ascent on Gimmer Crag in Langdale, which I remember finding very hard because the equipment for mixed winter climbing wasn't very good back then. We never dreamt of using two ice axes, for example, and the gear was still pretty rubbish. I now think that we shouldn't have done it because we shouldn't be spoiling classic rock climbs by marking the rock with crampons and axes.

About twenty years later, we decided to research our family name up in Edinburgh University library. As it turned out, my ancestors started a tradition of lead, copper, coal and iron ore mining, which later on got us into quarrying. We know from parish records and from church graveyards exactly when and where each ancestor was born, married and died, right through from 1700. One of them was mayor of Guisborough in North Yorkshire, and had a street named after him.

Since I'm on about family history, there's a fascinating story on my mother's side as well. A few years ago we were in a restaurant in Chamonix Mont Blanc in the French Alps and an American couple were struggling with the French menu, so we helped them out and got talking. He was mayor of Salt Lake City, but he had been a rock climber in Yosemite in California in the early 1960s. He had also camped illegally in the woods in Chamonix as a young climber in the 1950s and 1960s, just as we had, and so our paths had probably crossed. He had just been to a reunion at an international climbing school in Switzerland where he had once worked. We knew a few of the same international mountaineers and had a lot in common, so we agreed to meet the next morning for coffee.

I asked him about his European roots. His ancestors had emigrated from north-east England in 1840 on the sailing ship *Sea Breeze* from Liverpool. About six generations ago, a tough old woman called Simpson had taken her four youngest children on a classic wagon train across America to Salt Lake City. Now, my mother's maiden name was Simpson, and the *Northern Echo* had just published a big story about American Mormons who had been researching their roots. It turned out that this formidable old battleaxe had emigrated with the four younger children while her husband had chosen to stay behind with the four older children. This guy was descended from one of the younger children in America, and I was descended from one of the older ones that stayed behind with the father. We were distant relations, descended from the same adventurous woman and with similar climbing interests, and mixing in similar circles. It's a small world.

Later on, when I climbed the North Face of the Eiger in Switzerland with a mate, I remember that my mother told the other women in her Ladies' Tea Club that it was my brother who had climbed it, even though it was not – he wasn't even there. I don't think I ever got any credit for anything within the family. Maybe that's what my motivation was.

Things changed dramatically when, at fifteen years old, I led a new pitch in Langdale that none of the other lads could do. Similarly, the first time at Stanage on gritstone I led a climb that the other lads couldn't lead, and that started to transform my confidence. Climbing propelled me out of my shyness.

I've never really thought about it, but I suppose I didn't have a great relationship with my father and I was quite pleased to leave home at eighteen and go off to university in Nottingham. I remember having to moderate my north-eastern dialect because most of my new acquaintances were from 'down south' and couldn't understand a word I said.

Another old pal from these days now tells me that our mates used to stop me outside on purpose and keep me talking to see if I got cold, because coming down from the north, I apparently ran around everywhere in just a T-shirt, even in winter.

Peter in *The Vent*, Cairngorms. © Peter Allison Collection

Chapter 2
ICE CLIMBING DEVELOPMENT

After that first trip to the Austrian Alps as a schoolboy in 1957, we started to go to other alpine areas, travelling by bus, train, hitching, motorbikes, vans – anything.

By the late 1950s we were going to the Dolomites, because I suppose we thought of ourselves as rock climbers, but we also diverted to Zermatt to have a look at the big mountains. We drove a van right up the private Zermatt track to the village at night and got the camping gear out, then realised that was illegal and took the van back down the valley and walked back up. We camped in a field behind the railway station because that was the bottom of the village then. Now it's in the middle of the village as Zermatt is so heavily built up, mostly with jewellery shops.

We soon realised that rocky mountains in that area are mostly loose limestone and mostly falling down. Consequently, we carried a week's worth of food up to the Schönbiel Hut about 3,000 metres above Zermatt and sat there until the weather improved. We wanted a mixed rock and ice north face, so when the weather cleared we went across and climbed the north face of the Dent d'Hérens. Since then I've skied down underneath it many times, doing the Haute Route, and often wondered how we inexperienced kids managed to survive.

After that we went to Chamonix for the first time, where the rock is granite and much better quality. We did the East Face of the Aiguille du Grépon – a great classic. Then we felt we were ready for a Chamonix mixed snow and rock route, so we walked up to the Albert Premier Hut and crashed out under some boulders.

The next morning two English old codgers came out of the hut dressed in felt hats and plus fours. I think one was Edward Whymper. One of them certainly looked like the wooden carving of Whymper outside the Monte Rosa Hotel in Zermatt. So we followed them up the glacier and on to the snow slopes on the north side of the Aiguille du Chardonnet to do the *Forbes Arête*. They must have thought that we were young rock tigers because they let us climb past them on the rocky bits. Mind you, we only had a short bit of rope so we ended up climbing together at the same time. They might have thought we were fit, but more likely they thought we were incompetent and reckless.

The descent gully off the summit now has a long abseil, but interestingly, I don't remember an abseil that first time. We just slithered down a snowy gully. Since then I've climbed the Chardonnet lots of times, including soloing the *North Spur*, but I've always had to make one abseil in descent. Have the mountains changed or is it the memories of youth?

In those days, even the descents were epics. Torch batteries only lasted for an hour or two. We were invariably slow because of carrying too much heavy gear and brewing up a lot, so we were nearly always descending in the dark. We had no money, so all descents were on foot, usually lost, floundering down through trees and always clapped out.

Anyone who ever did it in those days will remember the midnight descent down from Montenvers to Chamonix. In the dark we would stumble down the path that seemed to traverse horizontally, so when you came to the railway line that descended gradually it seemed a better bet. However, partway down the railway line you came to a tunnel and you could see even less inside there. The torches were inevitably flat by this point. We all scraped an ice axe along the wall for some kind of contact but there were potholes so you'd stumble about, getting frustrated. Then when you came to a second tunnel, there was a gap down through the trees that promised better things. So we'd head straight down through the trees, getting into a mess and a foul temper. Then there was a drop off and a crag in the way. So we all did the same thing, in the same place, time after time. We got the rope out and abseiled from tree to tree, slip-sliding about in the dark and getting even more knackered and angry – angry with ourselves and angry with our mates. The epic turned into a nightmare.

Eventually you got down to your illegal campsite in the woods, with a plastic sheet over the leaky bit of your tent. The next day, the police came to evict you and clear away the dirty squatters. You promised yourself you'd give up alpinism and sell your gear. Next night you'd go to the pub and after a couple of beers say to your mate, 'Right. Which dangerous north face are we going to do next?' And here we are, some of us, sixty years later.

I hitched across Switzerland with a guy from Newcastle, sleeping in barns full of hay and cows. We liberated a few bags of apples from an orchard and eventually walked up a remote valley for about six hours in the rain and thick cloud. We thought we could shelter from a thunderstorm in a wood by a pond, but frighteningly I was knocked clean off my feet by an air blast as lightning struck the water. We were lost, of course, and eventually crashed out under some big boulders. After three days, the rain stopped, which was good timing because we'd eaten all the apples. We peeked out and there to one side was a posh Swiss mountain hut and to the other side was a great big rock face with new snow on the top and the summit in cloud: the north face of the Piz Badile.

By the time we'd put my big brass primus stove back into its tin box and dried out a bit we were only about fifth and sixth on the face, but even though I climbed in big heavy workman's boots we soon climbed past most of them. They were all smart continentals who had stayed in comfort at the hut and they climbed up pitons and wooden wedges hammered into cracks and then stood in slings. We were quite reasonable British rock climbers and couldn't be bothered with aid climbing. We were soon second on the climb, but I couldn't get past the first bloke, who was German. With the war still relatively fresh in people's minds, we were not popular with German climbers and vice versa. This guy was struggling. He was knocking rocks off and screaming at me and eventually fell off on to my head. I got a bit upset with him, and in the end I clipped a twist of his rope into one of his iron karabiners – just to safeguard him, you understand – but it gave him something to think about and we soon romped ahead. I'm a bit ashamed of myself. Near the top we were caught out – as just punishment and retribution – in my first big Alpine storm, with minimal bivouac gear. Feet and legs went into our heavy canvas rucksacks, and my 'secret weapon' then was a plastic Pac-a-Mac. This was a completely waterproof plastic coat that was fine under a boulder, but they weren't designed for wind, sharp rocks or ice axes and were diabolical within three metres of crampons. Ours were quickly ripped to shreds and we were soaked and plastered in snow.

In those days we never dreamt of carrying a heavy, ex-army sleeping bag for bivouacs and we didn't have down-insulated jackets. Really it was usually just an extra jumper, and nothing we had was waterproof. It wasn't until about 1965 that we got down jackets and gear became a little better. The gear nowadays is fantastic in comparison.

This was also my first experience of hair standing on end from lightning strikes and of skin tingling with the static electricity. We were often soaking wet in those days, of course, because of the lack of anything waterproof. In fact, the clothing we did have was quite good at keeping all the water inside. Apparently water and lightning don't mix too well … or rather, the opposite is true. Lightning flashes are very much attracted to water. Later on in life I would have mountaineering friends who had been struck and had burn marks on their body, occasionally in two places: where the lightning had struck and where it had exited. I remember finding the charred remains of a serious victim on the Dent du Géant.

Anyway, we got to the summit the next day, but we couldn't see anything. We had obviously been way off route after the storm, on tricky ground near the summit with snow and verglas ice coating all the rocks, and it had taken a long time to climb. This was all long before the idea of abseiling back down routes with modern, efficient abseiling gear and, inevitably, we somehow descended into the wrong country, never mind the wrong valley. The truth is that we probably didn't have a clue where we were. It's mountaineering instinct to know that you just have to get off the hill and down into the valley. So we set off again, uphill, to cross the frontier pass from Italy, get back into Switzerland, and face the long hitch-hike back home. I learnt quite a lot, quite quickly, about Alpine mountaineering.

During the early 1960s, I climbed in the Alps a lot with my elder brother. He was very pushy and ambitious to get his name in the guidebooks, but I was never interested in that. I just enjoyed the climbing. Understandably, we didn't get on all that well. We had absolutely no climbing or mountain-eering background in the family, but I suppose there must have been a bit of adventure somewhere in our genetic make-up.

We climbed on one thirty-metre, hawser-laid, three-ply nylon rope, and tied on to each end with a bowline knot directly around the waist (harnesses were still a long time from being invented). We abseiled down ropes by passing the rope under one thigh and back up over the opposite shoulder and then held the dead end of the rope, maybe with a twist around the fore-arm if it was steep or overhanging. Belaying was similar with the rope around the shoulder or waist, and again with a twist of rope around the forearm. The friction was desperate, and many climbers of my age have the rope burn marks to prove it. Somebody fell off on to me on the flake of *Central Buttress* on Scafell while I was using an old-fashioned shoulder belay, and the rope burns went through about three layers of clothing.

On belay stances in the Alps, my brother and I didn't care to spend too much time together. I used to tie him off to an anchor and take whatever slings we had, then just keep climbing. I'd put in a runner now and again and shout for him to start climbing. Then I'd just carry on until I ran out of slings. He'd come up to a stance and say, 'My, that was a long pitch.' Often we did sixty- or ninety-metre pitches. We were soloing really, but I don't think he realised that, and it allowed us to do some fairly quick ascents for Alpine routes at that time. It's just been re-invented now and called 'simultaneous climbing'. It's regarded as something modern and fast with several good modern runners between you, but we were doing it as young lads in the 1950s, although mostly for all the wrong reasons.

Early alpine ice climbs were even more precarious during this period and up until about 1966. Again, we had about thirty metres of rope between us, tied on with bowlines around the waist. The ice climbing gear consisted of old ten-point crampons bodged up with wire and string; cold, single-leather, curly Co-op boots; one straight wooden ice axe; woollen mittens; one twelve-inch-long, homemade iron spike piton each (sharpened at one end and a ring at the other end), and a one-and-a-half-pound builder's lump-hammer hanging from a string. And, the essential ingredient: big calf muscles from cycling a fixed-gear bike.

We could climb big Alpine faces of ice at up to sixty degrees and Scottish gullies of maybe seventy degrees, so long as we could bridge the feet out across a gully a bit. The technique was to chop footsteps with the axe and on steeper ice to chop a handhold as well. If the temperature was right a woollen mitt would freeze into the handhold and with a bit of luck the woollen jumper sleeve would freeze on as well for a bit more purchase.

On rock you only have holds where the rock decides, but in old-fashioned ice climbing you could chop holds wherever you wanted – providing you were strong enough. It was a balance of strength and plenty of holds, or boldness and not so many. We had to chop a big foothold for a stance, hammer in the iron spike and clip in with a big, heavy, steel, ex-war-department karabiner. Belaying was wrapping the rope around the waist and hoping that nobody fell off. We didn't have any runners unless it was mixed rock and ice climbing, with a few intermittent slings draped around a projecting rock spike.

The hard part was to then chop a great big hole in the ice each time with the straight wooden axe in order to get the only belay peg out. Your belay anchor came from stamping a long wooden axe into the hard pack, putting the rope around it and hoping for the best. One trick in those days was to have hard-boiled eggs in your pockets as hand warmers. As an added bonus you got to eat them when they went cold.

By about 1964 we had already done quite a few good north faces like this, with just basic gear: the Aiguille de Triolet, the Tour Ronde, the Aiguille d'Argentière, the *Frendo Spur* on the Aiguille du Midi, the *Route Major* on Mont Blanc, and the Aiguille de Leschaux – which hadn't been climbed since Cassin's first ascent, twenty-five years earlier – among others.

By then we'd also done some good mixed climbs as well, like the *Walker Spur* on the Grandes Jorasses, and some of these had been first or early British ascents.

When we were kids, the winter in north-east England and the North Pennines was either deep snow or slush. In the Lake District and Scotland, the ice on streams was thin and usually cracked just as you were walking over it. We had absolutely no idea about alpine ice on mountain faces in those days.

Once when we were pushing our luck on some alpine north face or other, we suddenly came across a 300-metre section of very hard black ice near the top. Our short holidays were always in late July, which isn't the best month for ice climbs, certainly not nowadays. This ice was rock hard and it was like chopping footsteps up a slope of cast iron. Our ice axe soon went blunt and I remember counting twenty-eight chops for each footstep. There was no alternative. We had rubbish belays, thirty-metre rope lengths, no runners and bodged-up crampons. I remember it took us over seven hours to climb up that particular 300-metre section and we were absolutely exhausted. I was physically sick three times on that route.

I never realised that the great Armand Charlet actually lived at the foot of these big alpine faces. He sat there while conditions were difficult and waited for about three days after each snowstorm until the new snow had transformed into nice crisp névé. Then, he probably romped up without cutting any steps.

As a youth, Joe Brown was a bit of a hero to us as he'd done so many great climbs on gritstone – and Tom Patey was another. Patey's own folk songs that he sang in the evenings while we all camped illegally in the

Chamonix woods, were hilarious. Brown and Patey did the second British ascent of the *Frendo Spur* on the north side of the Aiguille du Midi, being the British master on rock together with the British master on ice. As we were camped alongside them under plastic sheets we wondered if we were good enough to do it, so a few days later we went and climbed it and found out that indeed we were.

By 1964, I was carrying a sharp dagger-like spike in my left hand on ice routes, and stabbing the ice for extra purchase and then cutting one bigger footstep about seven feet up. The idea was to dice up into this step using better crampons with front points. I would hold the straight axe by the head with a sort of twist to stop the straight pick from popping out. This was all very precarious on big ice faces with dodgy runouts. But then I realised that if the pick was angled down a bit like the left-hand dagger it wouldn't slip out quite so easily. By the time we did the first British ascent of the Lenzspitze north face in 1966, we just drew a dotted line on a postcard picture and followed that straight up to the summit. We didn't know that the earlier ascent had gone across on to the left-hand ridge.

On the face I was using a hammer with a long thin pick that roofing slaters used then, and I'd bent the pick down between two big rocks and used that in my left hand. Unfortunately, the pick then snapped off. When we got home I modified an old wooden axe by sawing off part of the shaft and hacksawing off part of the adze, then bending down the pick into a curve using an oxyacetylene burning torch. This modified ice axe, from 1966, is still hanging on my wall, but I used it all the time between 1966 up until about 1972. I didn't chop as many footsteps on ice climbs after that in 1966.

History books say that MacInnes in Scotland and Chouinard in America thought of this first, but history has always been written by the scribes and not by the blokes that actually did stuff. The history of battles was always written for the winners. The other side may well have written different versions, if only they hadn't been dead. Either way, there's an old sepia picture of Andreas Hinterstoisser – of Eiger fame – in the 1930s, and he had a drooped-pick ice axe even then.

In 1967 we did the first all-British ascent of the *Couturier Couloir* on the Aiguille Verte. Then we went around Switzerland looking for north faces that hadn't had British ascents, again dotting lines on postcards and trying to tick them off. By this time, it was exhausting chopping these twelve-inch-long iron belay spikes out of the ice, and so I was making shorter ones from square rods and eventually from steel tube about three quarters of an inch in diameter and only seven or eight inches long. They were easier to chop out but obviously not as secure, so I hacksawed 'shanks teeth' notches along the sides and edges. However, we still only carried one each. It was always a compromise between security and hard work.

During this period, I guess there were only a few Brits doing these sorts of Alpine routes. In fact, there weren't many continentals doing them either, and so for a few years I was on the committee of the Alpine Climbing Group, which was a splinter group of the British Alpine Club. I always felt that 'ACG' after your name was more important than 'BSc'.

Several years later ice pegs were starting to improve, with screw threads and tubes. Some could be hammered in and then screwed out. Some designs were useless and wouldn't get the cork out of a wine bottle. Then Russian climbers started to make ice screws out of aircraft titanium tubes. They would screw in with a bit of leverage from an ice axe, and then screw out by hand. Unfortunately, all these things needed two hands, so it was usually necessary to chop a big foothold to get belayed. I fitted wire handles to these things to get the leverage. Nowadays we have fancy alloy ice pegs that fly in and out of the ice in seconds. In good solid ice they are even strong enough to hold a falling bus.

I still think it's a bit like doing *Cemetery Gates* in the Llanberis Pass. I've always said that if you can do *Cemetery Gates* you can do it in boots, or even in wellies. It's the same on ice. You don't really need the modern shaped, technical axes for the medium grade, classic alpine routes – they can even be a hindrance if you need to plunge an axe into softer snow.

On the subject of doing the *Gates* in wellies, I remember once being at a Climbing Club dinner in the Lake District when I had no time or intention of going climbing. But it was winter and conditions were very good, so I borrowed some crampons and strapped them on to my old wellies and plodded up a couple of easy gullies. You can't afford to miss the good, fine days out on the hills.

Peter's last car was a Maserati.

Chapter 3
MOTORCARS

Despite being expelled on the last day at school for making explosives in the lab, and considering I was listening to Radio Luxembourg all the time while fiddling results for physics experiments, I got surprisingly high marks. At the University of Nottingham I seemed to sail through first-year exams, so in my second year I spent all my time climbing, playing rugby and rowing. There might have been a wee bit of partying as well, but the rest of the time was spent fiddling about with motorbikes and old bangers.

On Friday nights I would try to put weight on for Saturday's rugby, usually in the pub, and on Saturdays I'd try to lose weight for climbing on Sundays, and usually other days as well. Being naughty boys, we climbed a lot on buildings with a series of good gymnastic routes on bridges and university buildings. If we got caught we'd say we were from the University of Sheffield and do a runner. Once, we finished up in Bolton and I climbed the town hall flagpole using prusik slings, and tied the inevitable underwear to the top. We joked that they couldn't possibly kick the whole second year department out, but of course they did, or at least one third of us were failed. Fortunately, a few of us were allowed to resit the whole year.

I would have no grant and no money as usual, so I worked three jobs that summer – six days a week on a building site, a Sunday ice cream van job and various evening pub jobs. I then got a very cheap attic flat in Nottingham next to a railway embankment and shared the rent with a good climbing mate who'd also failed second year exams. I saved enough money to pay resit fees and just about survive – but only just. In the cold winter of 1961, with no heat, we used Icelandic sleeping bags and duvets and had ice on the bed covers, never mind on the inside of the windows. Food was old loaves of stale bread left in halls of residence kitchens, fried in lard. Not very healthy, but excellent training for winter alpinism.

By my final year at university, my young brother, who was quite gifted mechanically, began modifying old motors extensively and making them much quicker but probably less safe. About this time an older climbing friend had a stag do in North Wales. It was raining, of course, and somebody decided to carry a rusty old metal table from outside the pub back to our campsite. He got tired and so I happened to be carrying this rusty lump just when the special constables jumped out on us, ranting about students and traffic cones on top of Tryfan. All my supposed mates slowed to give my name and address and so it was me 'wot got done.' The court case was in Betws-y-Coed, for petty larceny. So as we approached Betws later on, in my souped-up old banger with bean tins for an exhaust and climbing friends hanging out of the windows heckling, I asked an old lady in a tweed skirt for directions to the court. It turned out that she was the magistrate, but after going on about 'charming young man' and 'splendid defence,' she still fined me ten quid. The supposed mates didn't offer to pay their share, and I certainly didn't have a tenner. After a few days of climbing, on the way back to Nottingham it was pouring down again and the only windscreen wiper failed, so we worked it with a piece of string, side to side through the open windows. We couldn't see, of course, and finished up in a ditch and hitched back. I must have hitched tens of thousands of miles in those days, often after breakdowns, and sometimes intentionally. The trick was to stand at roundabouts with a university scarf and a rolled umbrella, and to try to look clean and respectable.

During my undergraduate days, a chemical engineering student who was a bit of a petrol head and myself also had half shares in an old Alvis Speed 20. It cost us next to nothing to buy, but that's because it was an absolute wreck. It needed half a gallon of petrol poured in the carburettors and half an hour of cranking the starting handle to get it fired up. We could only ever get it as far as the Rose and Crown and usually couldn't get it back.

However, this mate had a rich father who apparently had a four-and-a-half litre, 1928 supercharged Bentley. They're worth an absolute fortune now, but his had a cracked engine block. One day he rushed into my room and said they'd located a scrapped one that had an engine in it, so we went together to this remote farm in Nottinghamshire. This farmer dragged open some big barn doors and several chickens flew out of this big old heap of junk. It had no canvas roof and the body was rotten and rusty, but it was a 1928 supercharged four-and-a-half litre Bentley – or at least it had been at one time. We inflated the trashed tyres and pushed it out and put some oil in the engine. Then we wired up a battery from a tractor, cranked it over a bit and checked the spark plugs to see if there was a spark. After a lot of shouting and swearing we couldn't believe it when the beast actually started. I drove it along a farm track a bit, but the steering seemed kind of loose and we couldn't get all the gears. We had no tax or insurance or anything, but after wiggling a few things we decided to give it a go. Rather, my mate decided that I would give it a go.

We set off on the road back to town. We soon rattled along with the old speed needle darting about between thirty and seventy, although that could have meant anything. Eventually we got back on to University Boulevard, which is a tree-lined dual carriageway with quite a long straight. With foot hard down and with smoke coming out from everywhere we eventually saw the needle flicker up to 100 and I braked hard for the next roundabout. Unfortunately, the brakes weren't very good and only worked on one side. I guess rats had eaten through one side after thirty years in a barn, because the thing lurched sharply to one side and when I released the brake it lurched scarily the other way. We lurched from side to side, dabbing at the brakes and losing speed by scraping along the kerbs, until we eventually bounced around the roundabout. These monsters used to race around Brooklands at 120 miles an hour back in 1928. His father sent a low-loader to collect the car and I believe he got professionals to change the engine into his own car, which is probably immaculate and worth hundreds of thousands of pounds now.

After leaving university I had a choice of three jobs to start on the Monday. I couldn't decide which one to take, so naturally I went climbing for the weekend in North Wales and tossed a coin in the pub on the Saturday night. I was supposed to be a civil or structural engineer of sorts and the coin decided on a job at Battersea Power Station. However, contracts made by tossing coins in pubs are non-binding and by the Wednesday I felt I wasn't going to get on with south London and asked for a transfer to Sizewell nuclear power stations in Suffolk.

While working at Sizewell in the early 1960s, there was an incident worthy of historical note. A bit of scaffold tube had been accidentally left high up in a sixty-metre blank wall of vertical concrete and it was going to cost a few arms and legs to rescaffold the wall to remove it. We laid some scaffold tubes on the flat roof and cantilevered them out a few feet over the side with ballast weights on the safe end. I abseiled off the tube down the wall, hoping the counterbalanced assembly wouldn't move, or at least wouldn't move much. The offending debris was removed and thus the new industry of 'high access' work using climbing techniques was invented, saving the construction industry a lot of money.

That summer I had hitched from Durham to Shropshire and walked up a long drive into a private estate near Ironbridge – the home of the historic cast-iron structure. A wiry old bloke with a monocle had opened a great barn door and there was what I had come to see. A pale blue 1933 Wolseley Hornet Special, with long low bonnet and coach-built aluminium body-work, big wire wheels and massive chrome headlights. Unfortunately, it had no exhaust system at all, and only ran on four of the straight six cylinders. In addition, the front offside, cart-spring suspension had broken and collapsed on to the chassis. I had no tax, no insurance, no lights, no exhaust and no suspension but that night I drove it 250 miles in the dark, back home to Durham.

I was working for an outfit that made you sign your resignation letter, undated, at the same time as you started. Then they could sack you easily without any trouble whenever they wanted to, just by filling in the date. A dirty trick from the real world of cutthroat business. I used to call it the DCM award, whether I was receiving it or, later on, handing them out. It's the 'Don't Come Monday' award.

I also hitched a lift down to Southampton and bought the first of several MGAs. That one was a black ex-police car used for chasing villains. It was on the early Michelin 'X' tyres that were new but designed for dry continental roads. The rubber was so hard that they lasted forever; but they were lethal on wet British roads, so I threw them away and fitted decent tyres made from competition rubber. After all, the rubber is the only thing keeping you on the tarmac.

After that came an MGA 'twin-cam', which was rare and much more powerful, but very temperamental. I worked on the engine and sorted it out so that it could keep up with the flashy new E-types on the newly opened motorways. Sadly, the engine was modified a bit too much; it became over-stressed and eventually exploded in a shower of hot oil and bits on the way to work early one morning.

I then went through a series of Austin-Healeys, Big Austin-Healey 3000s and the like, but soon I could afford my then ambition, which was an original Lotus Elite. Lotus only made 900 of them between 1959 and 1962, so mine was of course second hand in 1965. They had cost £900 new and had only been sold to celebrities and racing drivers, and they reckon that Lotus lost £100 on each one they sold. They were tiny, light, fragile, and a lot of trouble. Lotus actually stands for 'Lots of Trouble, Usually Serious'. But they were brilliant if you had the skills to maintain them and they were fantastically well balanced to drive.

I had a Norton 600 Dominator bike at the same time and regularly went down to the Lotus factory that was then in Cheshunt, North London, and came back with wheels tied to the sides of the panniers. One time at the factory, the development engineers had rolled out a prototype car in front of me. It was the new Lotus Europe, the first car with a mid-mounted engine in a central backbone chassis. They were sick as parrots because one side weighed twenty pounds more than the other side, on the four corner scales. They pushed me out of the way but I couldn't resist a poke around and they were much happier when I found a big chunk of heavy towrope in the passenger door pocket on one side!

By this time I was living in an upstairs flat in a big Victorian house in Liverpool, with a half-built motorbike upstairs. It was quite tricky, but very exciting, getting it back downstairs. I was supposed to be putting the pinnacles up on the Roman Catholic cathedral because they wanted a civil engineer with a head for heights, so I'd been transferred from Wylfa nuclear power station in Anglesey.

I was driving the Lotus through Liverpool one day in a bit of a hurry, and blasting away from traffic lights when I suddenly realised there was a police motorbike on my tail. I shot into a big wide-open roundabout knowing that his two tyres couldn't possibly keep up with the Lotus. As I searched around, it was flat enough to see in my mirror that he was cranked right over on his bike, and there were sparks flying up off his footrest, scraping the road. So I slowed right down and tootled up to the next traffic lights. He came up alongside me and stuck his helmet into my open window and said, with a great big grin, 'My, I enjoyed that! You're nicked.'

Talking about sparks from footrests, the Norton was a great bike. One day four of us were climbing on Dinas Cromlech in Llanberis Pass and two of us had no transport. So, always being up for a blast, I took one pal down to Wendy's cafe in Llanberis and came back up for the other two, in succession. After a few brews of tea the first one said, 'We had sparks from the footrest on one bend'. The second one said, 'We had sparks from the footrest on several bends'. And the third one, who I swear had premature, but temporary, grey patches in his hair, said in a shaky voice, 'we had sparks from the footrest on every bend'.

Of course, the bikes of the 1960s were nothing compared with the super-bikes of the present. When I bought a modern superbike, as a 'born-again biker', I first rode it around a big car park, in and out of parked cars, in a big figure of eight to get the hang of it, very gently. My son Simon, with me at the time, said, 'No! Dad, that's no good.' He then got on his big growling Yamaha, picked it up into a wheelie, rode around the same figure of eight circuit just on the back wheel, then rode alongside me, dropped it on to the front wheel, braked hard, lifted up the back end, swung it round through 180 degrees, parked alongside me, and said, 'That's how you do it.' I rest my case.

That's enough about mad motors and antisocial driving; let's get back to the climbing.

Peter leading *Brant Direct*, Llanberis Pass, May 1975. © Peter Allison Collection

Chapter 4
ROCK

I remember doing *The Sloth* at the Roaches as a teenager in the late 1950s in moleskin breeches and pumps and with only one runner, the locals jeering below saying that young strangers shouldn't be allowed to come and steal their plum routes.

When Don Whillans had done the first ascent he'd been smoking a cigarette, which he left half smoked in a flake handhold under the big overhang. When Joe Brown came up he took the cigarette and finished off smoking it. Joe had shouted up, 'Hey Don! There's a lot of slack rope down here,' and Whillans had shouted down, 'There's a lot of slack rope up here as well, Joe; shall I drop you some more?' When I did it, I swear there was still a part-smoked 'fag end' left in one of the flake handholds. It was still dry because the overhang kept the rain off.

I remember getting caught in heavy rain on the crux move of *Hangover* in the Llanberis Pass, climbing in second hand klettershoes. They were like a modern walking boot with a Vibram sole and a rubber rand around the side. They were about as delicate on wet, slippy rock as a wellington boot, but of course we were all 'stony-broke' in those days, and they were marginally better than Woolworths pumps. The cream of the climbing world were watching below on that occasion as well, getting wet and probably expecting a big fall.

I have also got to confess that it was our generation of students in about 1960 that bashed homemade pegs into the thin cracks at places like Millstone Edge quarry in Derbyshire. I think Lawrencefield Quarry was still completely overgrown with trees and ivy about that time. I made pitons from bits of angle iron, and thin ones from old bean tins. On rainy days in winter we would swing around for hours in slings, getting soaking wet. The upside of all this is that it created the little fingerholds in these thin cracks that has allowed the free climbing of some of today's finger-crack climbs.

However, those student days messing about with homemade pegs in winter made me quite dislike too much aid climbing, and so afterwards I very rarely carried pitons and always much preferred free climbing, even in the Alps.

In the early days, long before we developed nuts and chocks for runners, this policy sometimes left us rather deficient in the protection department with long runouts, but despite this the late 1950s and early 1960s were a golden age. We all knew everyone else on the crags, climbing at a high standard, and it was all very exciting with secret, mystical new crag 'X's, and the opening up of big new sea cliffs. I climbed with lots of different people.

I often did huge weekend drives both to Scotland and the Alps, but on one occasion when I was working in Suffolk, I drove 120 miles down to London at night to pick up a good climbing mate and then drove straight away back up to North Wales. We went directly to Tremadog in the early morning, without any sleep and went on a rock climb called *Barbarian*, which, in the early 1960s, used a piton for aid to surmount an overhang. Nothing must have happened for quite a long time because I suddenly woke up with my mate shouting up from below. I was bridged across a groove underneath an overhang with one finger securely locked through the eye of a peg. I had been fast asleep. I must have just 'dropped off.' For a power nap, I suppose.

I bought a little cottage for £550 at the Vaynol Estate auction in Snowdonia in 1967, and Denny Moorhouse opened his first factory next door, which eventually became DMM – a maker of climbing gear. We had both done similar routes in the Dolomites and so we talked about modifying nuts and making chocks and alloy wedges for runners, and improving pitons and karabiners etc.

I have only fallen off five times in sixty-five years while leading, which isn't bad, but one early fall was a real biggie. I had an improvised chunk of iron on a sling jammed in a crack underneath an overhang, about twenty metres above the ground, and nothing for protection on the wall above. The climb had not then been done and it got harder and more precarious higher up. After about another fifteen metres it got harder again instead of easier, and there was no way I could reverse the moves. Eventually I slipped off and went winging into space, but unfortunately, without the wings. My second, holding the rope with an old waist belay, had instructions to use a very dynamic belay, i.e. if I fell off he was to jump off his belay block and slither down the scree to take in some of the slack rope. I plummeted thirty-five metres on to a single bowline knot around the waist and left footprints in the mud. But the elasticity in the old nylon rope absorbed some of the energy and the chunk of scrap iron jammed in the crack and so had done its business. Remarkably, I hardly felt a thing and walked away unscathed, but I guess we both had a few bruised ribs the next day. However, this proved the efficiency of jammed nuts and their careful usage, and we went on to cut, shape and develop all sorts of chocks and alloy wedges on slings and then on pieces of wire. I even used little Meccano nuts on nylon bootlaces and bits of high tensile wire, tied up with knots and insulating tape.

In the early Gogarth sea cliff days, I went with a young Manchester lad, Mike, across to Holyhead in one of my TVR Rockets to do *Red Wall*. Suddenly, an old Morris 1000 Traveller slowed into the gravel car park and Ken Wilson leapt out with two young superstars in shorts and headbands and Ken shouted 'Whatyergonnado?' all in one excited word. I'd just taken Ken up *Primus*, a strenuous quality route, and he'd promoted me on his own team sheet into the 'A–' category. What an honour!

I told him where we were going, and he said, 'You can't, you can't. These lads went on it midweek and left some of their gear on it.'

I said, 'Come on, Ken. You know the score around here. First to the crag goes on the route.'

And then they came out with the great classic, 'Well, we left Llanberis before you, but you passed us on the road!'

I waited for a suitable pause, then said, 'Well, okay then. You can go first. But I hope you don't climb as slow as you drive.'

They went and abseiled right over the top of the crag, in balaclavas and full gear. I couldn't believe it. Then they went and dropped their coiled rope accidentally into the sea. We abseiled down the side of the crag the safe and sensible way and gave them a top rope to enable them to fish their wet rope out of the sea.

To the left of *Red Wall* there's a route called *Wendigo*, which was very loose and friable in the early days. I remember handholds snapping off above my head and dropping over my shoulder, counting the seconds until they dropped straight down into the sea, 120 metres below. Dick Isherwood did the third ascent and asked how I'd got up the steep blank wall in one pitch. I told him I put a little sling over a tiny knobble and stood in it. When I reached the next handhold the tiny knobble snapped clean off and fell into the sea. I also told him that Joe had admitted to me in the pub that on the first ascent he had stepped left and put a sling on a loose spike and used that.

Dick said, 'Thank goodness! We all cheated. I stepped right and put a peg in a crack and used that.' Now the climb has been cleaned up and the loose rock has come off, it's another one of the great three-star classics.

The early sea cliff climbing was hugely exciting and atmospheric with a cacophony of sound effects. There were the screaming sea birds and the crashing waves. There was the sound of the wind whistling around corners and the plop of loose rocks dropped over the shoulder straight down into the sea. Then there was the occasional swell of the Irish ferries. There was even the boom of the foghorn from the lighthouse. Very eerie.

In the early days at Gogarth a lot of the routes were loose or friable and poorly protected. Before the invention of harnesses and modern gear, many routes were intimidating and some just plain scary. We were doing a precarious route on the Main Cliff in about 1967 when a 'new kid on the block' appeared and did a new route up the top tier. He was Ed Drummond, and he called the route *The Strand* because it was a straight plumb-line crack. We actually watched from our top belay as he cleaned and climbed it, with only a little bit of 'jiggery-pokery'. It was a brilliant line just waiting to be climbed, on another great bit of rock. The trouble was that he wrote a letter, which we all read in the pub, claiming that it wouldn't be repeated for ten years and that it was graded 7b (whatever that meant). He had invented this grading system of his own that we all thought was rubbish at the time; but of course, it eventually became the standard way of grading the technical difficulty of a pitch. It was quite groundbreaking really and is an excellent system and now universally in use.

However, the 'wouldn't be repeated for ten years' bit was reminiscent of pieces of red cloth and male cows. Mike and I went back the following Saturday and repeated it. The crack was blind, the bits that weren't blind were full of mud, the other bits were friable and the whole thing was covered in the Gogarth 'wire-grass'. It had been a cracking achievement, a great line and now is another of the great three-star classics.

Mousetrap was also an intimidating route initially, but it's such a brilliant climb up a complicated chunk of rock in a stunning location. It is on everybody's ticklist; I did it several times with different people, including solo.

One weekend we were in the pub in Llanberis at lunchtime because it was absolutely lashing down with Welsh rain. The crags and hillsides were really wet. I was with a mate who would always agree to almost any kind of stupid idea while in the pub, and I suggested we go and mess about and see if we could get up *Cemetery Gates* in this kind of weather. We went in double layers of full waterproofs and boots and gave it a go, just for a laugh, which of course wasn't much of a laugh at all. The water was streaming down everything. It was pouring into my cuffs and down inside my clothes, and my boots were full and overflowing with cold water. I swear on my honour that I didn't pull on more than about twenty slings, and maybe my feet might have brushed against a few as well. But as they say, it's great when it stops.

At that time, I climbed a lot with Jancis, who later became my first wife. She was then the best British female rock climber, and the first to do *Vector*. Later on, she very commendably became the first female president of the Climbers' Club. Leo Dickinson early in his photography and film career took classic pictures of her when he joined us to do *Winking Crack*. (Joe Brown, who did the first ascent, said it always winked at him when he walked underneath it.) Jancis and I did a few things together on Cloggy and in Cornwall, and then a few early ascents on Gogarth. *Big Groove* and *Rat Race*, the five or six pitches of badly protected, friable rock, were quite stressful at the time. I remember sometimes not getting to the pub until 10 p.m., with nerves shredded and knuckles trailing on the floor having just led all the pitches.

When we did an early ascent of *Great Wall* on Cloggy, there were wet streaks on the crag, and a pal had just abseiled off. But there were dry streaks as well and I thought we'd give it a go anyway, just to have a look. On the top pitch, in the damp, I realised that the first few ascensionists had probably abseiled down first and bashed a peg into a thin crack to protect themselves, which the second would have then removed. But as usual I wasn't carrying any pegs, as I was too lazy to carry a heavy peg hammer. I only had a few Meccano nuts threaded on a bit of cord and I couldn't get any of them to jam into the crack. I couldn't get my fat fingers to jam into this thin crack either. There wasn't much in the way of handholds and a crucial toe hold was a bit damp; it was all getting a bit serious. I had no runner and no holds, and not a lot of hope. But there was this little peg hole in the crack and I could get a little finger into the hole and twist it sideways to lock it off. Okay, it's painful, but not quite as painful as banging your head on the rocks below at a million miles an hour after a 100-metre fall through space.

The toecap of my old rock boots was quite worn because of lots of climbing on rough gritstone and my toe was sticking out a bit, so it was slip-sliding on this damp foothold smear. Then, whoops! The side of the toecap split away, and the flap got in the way of trying to bridge across on the smear.

So with most of my weight on the little finger jam I tried to reach down and rip off the remains of the offending toe flap. It was a sort of bridging move, but it's quite difficult to bridge on just one leg while sorting out the other boot. Somehow, I stayed on the rock. A dodgy move at that moment and this memoir would have been a lot shorter. Of course, afterwards at the top, with my pulse back down below 300, I looked back down the crag and tried to persuade myself that it had all been 'just a wee doddle'.

About this time, there was a brush with thievery, which was most unusual. I was soloing about on Dinas Mot and had left my sack full of gear at the bottom of the crag. When I got down it had gone. Later that night I walked into the local pub that we all used at that time and shouted forcefully: 'Somebody has pinched my sack from the bottom of the Mot, and I want it back'. At closing time my sack and all my gear was left by the pub door, with a little anonymous note saying, 'Sorry! We didn't know it was yours.'

Gogarth sea level traverses were much more light-hearted fun and in a fabulous setting. Altogether I think we did about seven miles over seven separate days, right round from Trearddur Bay to Holyhead harbour. Sometimes it was an amble along easy rock ledges just above the sea. At other times we were soloing desperate moves twelve metres above the sea and there were pendulums and Tyroleans and slacklining and lots of epics, and lots of getting very, very wet. Most teams included a strong swimmer for getting a rope across the impossible bits, and a genuine cowboy was quite useful for lassoing spikes.

An amazing incident occurred when we soloed around a corner through a cave and met another team coming the other way wearing rock boots and helmets, but otherwise completely starkers – and the rock was very rough on that particular section. Once when we abseiled down into the middle of the Irish sea to explore, the wind blew the abseil ropes back up and we felt very compromised, with a big tide coming in. Nearly all of our mates of that era had many epics on sea cliffs, involving lots of getting very wet.

When we'd done desperate abseils in the old days with the rope around the thighs, and then later used figure of eight 'sit-slings', with the abseil rope over the shoulder, we'd often tried to figure out how to improve things. We'd experimented with different types of tapes and slings to try and make a sort of harness. Because so many regular 'seconds' had got rope burns from holding falling leaders using a waist belay, some of us began to improvise a crude belaying device. At first, we put a loop of rope through a second karabiner and clipped it in. But there wasn't enough friction. Then we put a little loop of the climbing rope through a single big 'link' cut from a length of steel chain, and clipped the loop into an old-fashioned steel karabiner: That gave us enough friction to abseil from and this eventually led to the early development of belay plates.

In the late 1950s we had already been through a phase of trying out differ-ent waist belts. The best had been several wraps of hemp rope around the waist tied off, and then a big steel ex-war-department karabiner to clip to the main climbing rope. For a while we had done this with a Tarbuck knot, which was a sliding friction knot, like a hangman's noose. If you fell off, this knot tightened on the karabiner and absorbed some of the energy. Some of us had even tried falling out of trees on to different sizes of nylon slings on branches, using this system, but it wasn't brilliant and most of the time we had just used the simple bowline around the waist. Then slowly, through the 1960s, a climbing harness was developed made from webbed tape, and ropes and better slings were developed. Later, better protection nuts and chocks came along, and belaying improved enormously with a succession of different belay plates, devices and techniques.

I had a good relationship with Jancis and a great and successful climbing partnership, and we married and had two good lads, Martin and Simon. Martin I named after the Martins Bank before it was taken over by Barclays, and he was doing hard rock climbs even before he was born, if you know what I mean. But Simon was born seven weeks prematurely with a bit of a shortage of oxygen, and he struggled for quite a few years with all sorts of co-ordination and balance problems. However, he picked up completely by about nine years old. Then both of them did all the usual boys' things such as riding BMXs over neighbours' VW Beetles and north-eastern win-ter sledging inside fertiliser bags. They both learnt to ski by being towed up into the Northern Pennines behind Land Rovers in winter, wearing welling-ton boots and skiing down over snowdrifts, stone walls and dead sheep. By fourteen years old they were both skiing couloirs with me in Chamonix.

After working 'full on' back in the north-east for many, many years and eventually retiring down to North Wales, I got to repeat many of my earlier ascents of routes like *T.Rex*, *Left Wall* and *Memory Lane*. Then I got on to the slate, which I'd missed out on because of business, and did climbs like *Comes the Dervish, Flashdance, Jack of Shadows, Ride the Wild Surf,* and *Great Balls of Fire* – all brilliant routes and all with fabulous names.

I remember one particular day in the slate quarries doing *Poetry Pink,* which is graded E5 6b. You do a 5c move without falling off, because you'd hit the deck, then clip a bolt and do a 6b move, in my case scratching on by fingernails.

There was some new young hotshot who looked like a child, about six metres to my right, smeared in a totally blank scoop. He pulled his woolly sleeve down and plastered about a hundredweight of chalk on to his hand and sleeve and stuck it on to the blank rock. Then he just sort of mantled. He mantle-shelved up until he seemed to stand on top of his own arm. I reckon his woolly jumper was used as an artificial aid. After that, even old-fashioned me went out and bought a chalk bag and started going to middle-aged-men's stretch classes.

Before chalk, back in the 1960s, one old gun had invented something that he had called 'sticky fingers', but I think he had really just smeared EvoStik on his fingers for extra purchase. I don't think it had been very successful, but it was probably the start of people thinking of new ideas and techniques and, heaven forbid, even going training and building indoor climbing walls.

Peter summitting the North Face of the Eiger, 1974. © Dave 'Smiler' Cuthbertson

Chapter 5
THE EIGER DAYS

In our student days we had acquired some ex-army Ventile and Windcol material and had made our own pullover cagoules. They were close-woven cotton materials and the principle was that when dry they would breathe through the pores in the weave, and when wet the cotton would swell and close the pores, making it waterproof. But the reality was that after a bit of wear on gritstone crags they would soak up the rain on the outside and squirt it into the inside.

Originally our alpine bivouac gear had been an extra school shirt; and then a yellow oilskin cycle cape, but they were incredibly heavy. So then I tried a 'Pac-a-Mac' plastic cape that just shredded in contact with rock or crampons. After that the latest technology was a great big nylon bag.

When Gore-Tex first came out it had been developed for medical use. However, I got a sample of early Gore-Tex from America and sewed it up into a homemade anorak and tested it in torrential rain in the English Lake District. With this early homemade Gore-Tex coat I walked in a wool jersey until saturated and then put the coat on. After a while I felt inside and was quite dry – it had worked. Gore-Tex, like all the modern gear and materials, has totally transformed the sport of mountaineering. But we got into winter alpinism long before Gore-Tex was invented.

Previously, we had walked for hours uphill to do rock routes on the Dru in Chamonix. But after they built the top ski lift on the Grands Montets in 1967 we found a way of going around the top and getting across to the Dru that way; and when we did the north face it was absolutely plastered in snow and green ice. We got up into thick cloud, then up to the Niche and cut a ledge in the ice and bivvied to an ice peg. The next day when we got higher, we couldn't traverse right on to the easier ground because of the thick ice and all the snow. So we had to go straight up and climb the harder, more direct *Fissure Allain*, which is graded VI in summer when it's dry rock.

There was four inches of vertical ice in the crack and over all the rocks. We could see pitons and wooden wedges in the crack under the ice, but we couldn't clip into any of them. It was all pretty tricky.

Unfortunately, rocky pinnacles like the Dru and the Chamonix aiguilles warm up during the day, even in winter. A big mountain mass like the Matterhorn that sticks up into the sky in an isolated position does too. So when a bit of bad weather comes along they are surrounded by cold air and the heat transference changes just ordinary poor weather into really nasty weather.

Nasty, localised mountain storms can be really grim, especially in winter. They're best avoided. By the time we got to the summit it was snowing again, and after a few abseils down the south side the old nylon ropes froze up and we couldn't pull them down, so we bivvied again on a narrow ledge with our feet in slings and a nylon bag over our heads. Unfortunately, it snowed hard for two days and two nights, but we had plenty of water for brews because the spindrift kept trying to push us off the narrow ledge.

On the third morning the snow stopped but the doubled abseil ropes were now about four inches in diameter with ice. We tossed a coin, except we didn't have a coin, but whatever it was, I lost. (Would you rather be rich or lucky? Answer: lucky, every time.) So we tied one rope to our belay peg and I prusiked up the other rope with two thin slings, banging the ice off the rope above my head using my ice axe. It was very slow progress, and when I was about six metres from the abseil peg there was a sudden explosion of ice lumps and I started to fall. I thought for a moment that the abseil peg had come out and this was it. I fell about six metres, but stopped and clipped into one thin sling. The forty metres of rope on the other side had been untensioned because it was also jammed with ice, and when all the ice eventually shattered off the ropes, I had fallen the equivalent of the stretch in the other forty metres. When we eventually got down to civilisation after five days we fancied a drink, but of course we didn't have any cash.

This adventure was with my good friend Smiler when we were young, fit and bold. Much later on, he rescued two Japanese climbers from an alpine route and brought them back to our campsite. We gave them bacon butties and their eyes lit up at chocolate-chip biscuits. We thought they must be poor, but in appreciation they invited us all back to their campsite for a Japanese banquet. They didn't speak English, or at least not Smiler's 'Brummie' anyway, and our Japanese wasn't quite perfect – but they had a dictionary. The Brummie vowels weren't quite the same as Queen's English, so 'bad vowels' got translated as 'bad bowels'. They thought we were insulting their food.

On one occasion I went on the north face of Les Droites in very thin conditions, with two good friends. The idea was that two very poor belays about five feet apart would be marginally safer than just one very poor belay, and both seconds would climb together. We crossed the bergschrund at midnight when it stopped dripping and got cold, as I usually liked to do on ice climbs, and made good progress. We were halfway up at breakfast time with just the top mixed buttresses to do. Then one of the others suddenly talked of being poorly and of recent hospitalisation, which I had known nothing about. There was suddenly unrealistic talk of soloing down or traversing sideways, but the only sensible option was a very precarious and careful retreat. We downclimbed some steep slush over blank granite and abseiled from rattly rock pegs and half-in ice pegs. We abseiled from 'Abalakov' threads drilled into soft ice – probably before Abalakov was even born. It took us all day, but we all got down completely safely, across the bergschrund and down on to the glacier, all in one piece. Well, three pieces actually, but much better than six! I felt it was quite an achievement and a relief; again a shedload of experience gained very quickly.

I personally don't think it's a failure to turn back and retreat on a big mountain route. I've never understood Summit Fever: if you're knackered and can't go on, or conditions are just too dangerous, it's no good pushing on to exhaustion, and there's not a lot of point in dying. Turn back. You might feel bad for a bit but you'll soon feel better as you descend. After all, the only objective in my book is to survive.

Before weather forecasts were much good, I was halfway up a big north face with a mate and we were bivvied on a little ledge tied to a peg. At midnight the stars were twinkling really brightly, and I thought it would be brilliant weather the next day and we'd romp up to the summit. But much later I learnt a bit about meteorology and came to realise that excessively twinkling stars is due to a strong high-altitude wind that brings in different weather – quickly. By 3 a.m. we were in thick cloud, and by 4 a.m. we were in the middle of huge lightning flashes, both above and below us. We lowered the gear six metres but were still receiving electric shocks up the wet ropes, and yelping like wounded dogs. By 5 a.m. the lightning had passed over and the wind dropped, but the snow started, with great big flakes. By 6 a.m. everything was plastered white, especially me, as I rigged up the first of several very careful abseils.

I had been on the Eiger North Face when we were young, after doing the *Walker Spur* in 1964, and at that time had been suitably impressed: meaning suitably wowed and gripped. So I was up for another go in about 1970, this time with my pal Smiler. The face just happened to be in poor condition – mild and dripping – but we went up to have a look and bivvy at the Swallows' Nest. It's a good ledge under an overhang, nice and safe while you're actually sitting there. In the night the drips got worse and we knew that we were going to abseil down. Just as we started to retreat the whole of the second ice field avalanched from above us. Maybe just the front three feet or so went, and maybe it was just four or five feet deep, but a couple of hundred metres wide and a couple of hundred metres above us. Under the overhang, however, we were completely safe. We'd left a bit of spare rope across the *Hinterstoisser Traverse* because it was clearly not reversible, and then set off fixing alternate abseils down, knowing that everything loose above us had already fallen off.

As I slid down the abseil ropes in an icy chimney, there was my mate scraping at a glove in the ice. I had a chop as well and suddenly a boot sprang out of the snow, with a leg fastened to it. It had a broom shank inside old breeches, and I said 'Hey Smiler, Hermann the German's been soloing the Eiger with a wooden leg.' Just then he was tugging at a helmet saying, 'Our kid wants an 'elmet'. Then the whole head came off, with another broom shank stuck down into a jacket stuffed full of straw; and Smiler fell backwards on to the abseil ropes in shock and nearly knocked us both off. I had just seen the *Eiger Sanction* film starring Clint Eastwood so I had known straight away that it was the dummy that was supposed to be some kind of spy who had fallen off. He thought it was Sedlmeyer, one of the early pioneers who had fallen off. So did some American visitor, looking up through a telescope so enormous that he could see what we had in our sandwiches. We dined out on the story for several years.

Then later on we had a proper go at the 'Big E'. In the 1950s and 1960s our preparations for climbing were a long night in the pub wearing tight jeans and a baggy wool jumper, followed by a scary drive in a clapped-out van.

But this time we took preparations for the Eiger more seriously. The weekend before, we parked in Llanberis Pass and then in big mountain boots and with a proper sized rucksack, we went up and did *Nose Direct* on Dinas Mot, and then *Main Wall* on Cyrn Las. Then we went up to Clogwyn y Ddysgl and did a long VS climb there. Then we went up over the top of Snowdon and down to Clogwyn Du'r Arddu to do *Great Slab* in a bit of drizzle, and then up over Snowdon's summit again and down to Y Lliwedd for another long easy route, and finally over the top and back down to the car in the pass. That was five long mountain rock routes with full gear, about 760 metres of proper rock climbing, plus a fair bit of up and down as well. The next day we scrambled up the North Ridge of Tryfan to the top and came down and did it a different way, and then did it again. And again. That's quite a few hundred metres of up and down.

By then I was working back up in the north-east and there's a miniature Matterhorn called Roseberry Topping that's a couple of hundred metres above the road with a ring of little sandstone crags around the summit. So one afternoon and evening I ran up from the road and soloed a different little rock climb up to the summit, repeating this fifteen times as training – about 1,800 metres of vertical uphill with a couple of hundred metres of solo rock climbing.

The next weekend we felt ready, and drove out to Grindelwald and went straight on to the Eiger North Face again. As a teenage lad, I'd remembered walking up to do a rock climb that was quite hard and I had not been sure whether I was ready for it. I'd been quite nervous and apprehensive, and of course I failed on it. But on this occasion, walking up to the North Face of the Eiger again, I don't remember feeling the least bit nervous. We were fit and prepared. We had the right gear, but without having sacks that were too heavy. We were confident, and I like to think that we were skilled and competent.

I had telephoned Zurich Airport to get an accurate weather forecast in the Grindelwald area, and I knew details of most of the route. So we climbed up to the Swallows' Nest bivouac ledge in thick cloud and mist and stopped to make a good meal. We knew the weather was on the mend and as the cloud started to clear we looked up and could see a little glimpse of the Ramp, 600 metres above us, plastered in snow. There was a little patch of blue sky through the clearing cloud, almost enough to make a sailor a very small pair of trousers. In the evening, we shot up the First Icefield and the first two pitches of the Ice Hose to a little ledge in a corner, which I'd sussed out previously. Then we did the next difficult bit up on to the Second Icefield, which would have been very hard in the morning with verglas ice on the rocks. So we put in several ice pegs and left the abseil rope back down to our little bivvy ledge for the night. The thing is that 'timing is everything in life'. When you get a job. When you meet a partner.

There's nowhere where timing is more important than on the Second and Third Icefields on the Eiger North Wall. By late morning the sun loosens all those rocks in the ice near the summit and the bombardment of stonefall starts. If you sleep at the Swallows' Nest you'll be too late at the dangerous sections. Okay, the Swallows' Nest is comfortable and safe, but it's too low down. God has put it in the wrong place. As it was, with my plan, we could only get short 'power naps' on our tiny ledge, but by dawn we were up our abseil rope, and after several hours of motoring we were up to the Flat Iron section and then the so-called Death Bivouac. By midday we were across the dangerous last ice field, which is crucial, and safely into the Ramp. I had always wanted to climb it when frozen up in icy conditions with a minimum of stonefall, even though it meant climbing every single pitch in crampons. For us, the Brittle Crack was the hardest pitch. We tried it with crampons, then without crampons, and then with crampons again. The only serious stonefall was in the middle of the Traverse of the Gods, which is a three-pitch traverse with big overhangs above and big overhangs below, and with no runners. A rock came winging out of space and splattered on the rock about two metres away from me. I could smell the cordite in the splintered rocks, so I scurried back to the non-belay for a shake out.

The White Spider was in good nick for us, and we romped up and into the second gully from the left, to get into the Exit Chimneys. Unfortunately, we didn't quite get to the big comfortable bivvy ledge before dark and so we spent another night tied to a little uncomfortable ledge with feet over the edge in rucksacks and slings. The Exit Chimneys overall were really good climbing, though with a little bit of ice over the rocks it was like doing nice rock pitches on Tremadog, but wearing crampons we still counted twenty pitches more up to the top, which gives an idea of the size of the thing.

After the summit, the north-west descent ridge had a few inches of slush over loose stones over rock slabs, and felt really precarious. The west face, though, was plastered with snow and so we descended right down the middle. It felt like a bit less than forty-five degrees and we just sort of glissaded down it, facing out, and I thought it would be a really nice ski.

After a few drinks, we went around to Zermatt for a route and then on to Chamonix to chill out. Smiler hadn't done the north face of the Courtes, so we went up there to have a look at that. I couldn't decide whether to do the *Swiss Route* again, on the right side of the face, or to try the *Austrian Route* on the left side of the face, which neither of us had done. The bergschrund was easiest in the middle and so we crossed it there and just carried on climbing straight up from there, between the two established routes. We went up broken ribs and buttresses of rock and ice, and just kept going. For a bit of a laugh, we called it the *Welsh Route*, but as always, I never bothered to write anything up anywhere because there was no need to. We just climbed for ourselves. I always just climbed for the fun of it and the buzz of doing tricky things with good mates. I was never interested in publishing what we had done, or making records really.

We descended back down the north side of the mountain by the north-east slope. It's almost exactly forty-five degrees for 1,000 metres, and again I sort of glissaded facing out, with an ice axe brake. Once again, I thought it would be a fantastic ski if you could get it in perfect condition.

Peter soloing at Scugdale with son Martin in background, June 1985. © Peter Allison Collection

Chapter 6
SOLOING

Having started climbing by going up trees and scrambling up problems in a little old sandstone quarry as a kid, I'd always enjoyed soloing about. When I discovered gritstone, it was brilliant soloing up an easy climb and down the next easy one and working your way around the Yorkshire and Derbyshire edges. In the winters from 1960 to 1963 there were stacks of snow. Stanage was snowed up to five metres from the top. You could solo the *Unconquerables*, or at least the top bits, learn the moves, and jump off into the huge snowdrifts. This way, I suppose, we started to solo routes that were a bit harder.

By the mid-1960s, a few of us soloists had circuits in Llanberis Pass. I would regularly solo routes like *Shadow Wall*, *Spectre*, *Diagonal*, *Sickle*, *Ivy Sepulchre* and *Overlapping Wall*.

As a youth, my apprenticeship on alpine ice climbs had been with rubbish belays and no runners and precariously chopped footholds with a straight wooden ice axe. Then a lot of rock climbing had been on loose or friable rock with poor protection. Generally, with shoulder belays and then with waist belays, it was a good idea if the leader didn't fall off. All this was pretty much ideal mental preparation for a bit of solo climbing, and I suppose it just progressed from there.

In 1966 I must have climbed nearly every day of the year. In the evenings after work there was Frodsham and Helsby. Then later that year, when I moved to work near Sheffield, there were different gritstone crags every night. Stanage, Froggatt and a million others. There's so much to do on grit and lots of stuff that's soloable. I was supposed to be building bridges on the M18, so I guess a few of them are probably in slightly the wrong place. I was driving a competition TVR that was set up with low gearing for doing hill climb competition events. It would only do about 110 mph, but it would do that pretty much anywhere.

One Friday evening I went from Sheffield to the Llanberis Pass. I wandered up to the Cromlech carrying my old worn Masters rock boots, thinking about soloing *Sabre Cut* that I'd done lots of times before, or maybe even *Cemetery Gates*. But at the bottom, I just felt good and confident and set off soloing up *Cenotaph Corner*. I'd done the climb several times before, including in big mountain boots as a sort of daft alpine training. In those days I always felt that the day would come when I'd have to climb that sort of grade on a big mountain, in big boots and possibly in bad conditions. So it was all just practice for something difficult in the future. At the niche there was still a peg then, and a finger went through the peg, not for aid or anything but just to shake out a bit and stop and think. But then, within seconds I thought, 'Don't think. Thinking leads to loss of concentration. Just get on with it.' I just bridged up a bit, laid away on the finger jam to reach the good handholds past the crux, and cruised over the top. I still felt very calm while scrambling down the descent gully and then allowed myself to consider that more soloing was possible, if you just stay calm and composed.

On the Saturday I think we did something suitably loose and scary at Gogarth. Then on the Sunday I was supposed to be going back to work, but a pal wanted a lift down to Tremadog and offered 'tyre money'; so I couldn't resist. Again, I was fairly buzzing from the drive, and climbing well and confidently. I had already done *Vector* several times, including in double mountain boots, again as a sort of alpine training, so I just went up and soloed it.

Whatever the history books might say, I'm pretty sure that these were the first solo ascents of *Cenotaph Corner* and *Vector*, way back in 1966. In the 1990s, I soloed a few rock routes that were a grade harder, but mostly in the slate quarries, which are delicate or technical rather than strenuous, and that suits me better. However, by then the standards had risen, and it was quite common for people to solo that grade, and much harder grades.

When I was working flat out back in the north-east, I had lots of short Alpine trips, sometimes just for long weekends, and I soloed a good few routes. I did the North Spur of the Chardonnet in about an hour and a half because it is only five or six hundred metres vertically. If you're climbing slowly with ropes and gear and a companion there are a few tricky technical pitches, to avoid a threatening ice sérac. However, if you're on your own you can sprint up an icy gully underneath the ice cliffs in just ten minutes or so, and reduce the risk. In this way you can argue that soloing actually reduces the time taken and therefore reduces the mountaineering risk. Thirty and forty years later, that way of climbing the route has now become quite common.

Later, while guiding, I had a client for the Hörnli Ridge on the Matterhorn. This was on a Monday, having trained him on loose rock scrambling the previous week. All guides have agreed to do the Matterhorn only one-to-one because it's quite loose and fairly serious. In fact, for every day that I've spent on the mountain there's been an average of one death. One day there were none, but then on another day two Italians fell down the east face on the descent. I'd promised to guide another Hörnli Ridge on the Friday with a client of another guiding colleague, so I'd stayed up at the hut, and on the Wednesday, after all the Swiss guides had rushed out of the hut at 4 a.m. on the dot, I had hung around for a while, fit but a bit bored. So I went out and around to the north side, just to wander about and have a look.

I'd already done the bottom third of the North Face with a mate on a day when it had been very cold – about -20 °C. We had kept our duvet jackets on and kept climbing together while roped up, because the climbing there is a straightforward snow slope. It was so cold that day and the ice had been brittle, resulting in poor ice axe placements, so eventually we bailed out. It's a wise man that knows when to retreat. There are times in the mountains when you really need to just get a grip and press on, but it's a great 'lifesaver' skill to have, knowing when to retreat.

I had thought about just repeating that bottom third by myself, but I'd been up the Hörnli Ridge two days before and conditions were good. This Wednesday morning the ice was just right and I could see the rocks higher up were just nicely covered with frozen, crisp new snow. The North Face is a bit over 1,200 metres vertical, but I'd already climbed an icy chimney, crossed the bergschrund and romped up the lower slope – 300 metres done. Just 1,000 metres to the summit and I reckoned there were only a couple of tricky technical sections where careful crampon technique would be required.

So I traversed right and cramponed up into a long frozen gully/ramp and into the middle of the face and the more serious stuff. At every tricky step you traverse a bit right and then back up again. Up, then step right, and diagonally up again. Nice and carefully. Brisk but steady. Another step. Careful. Good crampon technique and two secure axe placements. Another 300 metres done. Then out into the middle of the face, good move, frozen over loose rocks. Good conditions. Stay calm. Concentrate. That's 600 metres done, and another 600 metres to go. When soloing big stuff, you just sort of switch into automatic mode, with internal concentration and no mistakes.

Although the Matterhorn is probably the most recognised mountain on the planet because it is so spectacular and elegant, most climbers know that it is in fact formed from a great pile of loose limestone held together by ice. If you want to climb it you'd better do it soon, before it all falls down. It's actually the trough of folded strata in many layers of folded limestone. The other, even looser, layers of rock have been scrubbed away by millions of years of erosion by repeated ice ages. What is left is loose rock. One side is flaky and the other side is slabby. On the north side there aren't really any decent belays and not many positive hand or footholds either. It's all ribs and snowy slabs; you weave from side to side to follow the easiest line.

Usually on alpine north faces there are lots of small stones whizzing down the face, and often big ones as well. I can tell you that stonefall on north faces is really scary. The only way to climb this north face safely is to do it briskly when it's cool, snowed up and frozen. Conditions and timing are everything. So on that particular Wednesday morning I was totally committed. I just kept going. Whenever there were trickier bits or steeper ground I traversed right then up again. Crampon up the frozen névé and avoid the bare, loose rocky bits. Romp up an easy section of nice frozen snow. Angle not too steep here. Out right then diagonally up left. That's 1,000 metres done. Only another 300 metres to go.

Well acclimatised. Feeling good. Calf muscles feeling it a bit – feeling it a lot, to be honest. But don't think about it. So only 300 metres to go, and most of the difficult sections are below. So concentrate even more. Another awkward step. Another ramp line. Back on to good névé and only a hundred metres to go. You can see the summit ridge now. Make sure the axes are secure. Then the occasional rock step where the midday sun has softened the ice near the summit. Crampon points grating. Step up on to the top in the middle of the long summit ridge.

Carefully sit down in the snow. Legs over the side. Sod the view – I've seen it before, lots of times. Feel the pulse. Calm the heartbeat. Reap breaths. Drain the last of the flask. Totally forget what you've just done. You're on a big hill and accidents nearly always happen on the descent. Carefully along the summit ridge to the little bronze Madonna and the start of the Hörnli descent. And now there are other climbers to negotiate … but you're still on your own.

The Matterhorn North Face is not particularly technical or difficult, but it must be an absolute nightmare in bad conditions. But thoroughly frozen up covered in nice névé snow with crampons and two good ice axes, it was okay, and best climbed quickly, fast and light, and safely. That's how I'd always wanted it. By being there all week and climbing the mountain three times that week, that's how I got it.

I never came back and bragged about soloing the north face. I doubt if I said anything to anyone really. I just did it for myself. Actually, it's the mountain activity that I've always thought that I was best at. Climbing alone and briskly up mixed alpine faces that are not too technically difficult. I think that climbing is an intensely personal thing and I suppose a bit self-ish. There was no point in talking about it. Close family would just worry. Business friends wouldn't have a clue what I was talking about – eyes would glaze over. Some climbing mates would say you're mad and others wouldn't really understand. So there's no point. Just do it for yourself. It's important to feel content with yourself, within your own skin.

In 1964 I'd done the *Walker Spur* on the Grand Jorasses with my brother, and I'd always fancied doing the *Croz Spur* as well. During our ascent of the *Walker Spur* we went straight up the glacier past the derelict pile of wood that had been the original, avalanched Leschaux Hut. This was because we could see that there were two people there and we didn't fancy any haste, or daft kind of race. So we had gone up and bivvied in a grotty gully about three metres above the bergschrund. At 5 a.m. the next morning, two head torches came up the glacier like proverbial rats up a drainpipe. They were coming like the clappers and I thought that there was no way they'd get in our way – in fact, they'd leave us in their wake – so we didn't bother to rush to get started. We just lit the primus and had a brew.

Then suddenly the head torches went off to the side and started climbing up over to our right. When it got light, higher up, we could see them climb-ing the snow slopes up to the Central Couloir, with what looked to me like vertical rubble above. Then as we got higher, doing our usual sixty-metre pitches on a thirty-metre rope, there was a sudden tumble of whizzing rocks down on to them and their ropes were clearly cut. I remember being quite surprised because they just tied the bits together and carried on. I suppose they couldn't have abseiled down past all their knots anyway, but whatever, I was very impressed as a young lad.

We had the climb completely to ourselves with no one else on it, and very few pegs in those days. Mind you, that might have been because we had no description and just followed our noses all day. We got to the top in about eleven hours, which wasn't bad for those days with heavy gear and clumsy boots. In fact, it was many years before some 'fit bits' came and did it quicker.

It's a long time ago now – fifty-five years – but I recall that there had been some brilliant pitches in the middle section that weren't very hard and that lower down there'd been some icy sections that needed a few chips with the wooden axe. Higher up there'd been some quite tricky pitches on steep verglassed rock, but there'd also been some loose stuff and a few bits of stonefall – scary as always.

However, unfortunately, on the summit we hadn't a clue how to get down, back then. We didn't know if we could descend from the Pointe Walker, so we traversed along the ridge for a bit over other summits, then just set off down into Italy and eventually collapsed in a heap for a kip. We had just enough energy left to open, using an ice axe, a tin of Pemican that I'd carried all day. It was a sort of dried meat that had been used on the Antarctic expeditions and I think we must have found it somewhere. We heated it up on the primus and then made another brew that we drank from the empty tin.

When we eventually staggered down to the valley, we thought that we'd have to walk up to Helbronner and all the way down the Vallée Blanche back to Chamonix. But we were suddenly grabbed by some Italian guides and given the third degree. We thought we were going to be arrested and locked up for being young foreigners who had stolen one of their plum routes without their permission and before their young guns had done it. Where had we been? Who had we seen?

Then suddenly we were whisked up in the lift, for free, and shoved into the inner sanctum. The two head torches with the shredded rope had, in fact, been their superstar hero Bonatti and his mate. His wife and Italian colleagues were there and when they heard that their hero was still in one piece, we were suddenly heroes as well. The little bubble lift that goes across the Vallée Blanche, which had just been built in 1956, had been closed because of bad weather, but it was miraculously opened just for us, and we got a complimentary lift back, right over to Chamonix. Wow!

So I had a bit of a history on the Jorasses, and when I had an urge to solo the *Croz Spur*, I stayed quietly at the new Leschaux Hut and then negotiated the crevasses on the Leschaux Glacier nice and carefully. My attempt was however short-lived, because partway up the route there were rocks coming down the size of houses. I thought if I pushed on I wasn't going to see old age, and quickly came to my senses. I always carried a thin rope when soloing in the Alps, and I carefully bailed out.

Once, after soloing an alpine route and descending by the ordinary route, I came down to a big bergschrund with about a six-metre jump, which I've never been bold enough to do. The snow was very slushy, so I cut a huge mushroom bollard three metres in diameter in the slush and maybe a foot deep. Then I put my rope around it packed with plastic bags full of snow to stop the thin rope from cutting through. Then I abseiled over, very gently, just as the thin rope slowly cut though the slush bollard and lowered me gently down. Phew! Most soloists either have an accident or a big scare and stop. I think that most are only half-conscious of their motivations.

Before I finish this chapter I think it deserves a few more words about *what* and *why*? And *wherefore*? Is solo climbing justified? Well, how do you justify mountaineering, or motorbikes, or BASE jumping? The answer is that if you don't know, then you can't. It's up to the individual. If you can, you will. If you don't want to, then you won't.

At home in the Alps. © Peter Allison Collection

Chapter 7
SKIING

My first attempt at skiing was as an inebriated student in a field one winter, wearing wellington boots and using old wooden skis off somebody's ornament wall. It didn't go well.

The only way to climb in winter in the Alps is to ski. Back then snowshoes were useless, and anyway, what's the point of trudging down steep snow on tennis-bats if you can whizz down on skis? So we went to Cervinia on the south side of the Matterhorn to improve. Unfortunately, we couldn't do a decent snowplough turn between the whole lot of us, so we decided that we were ski mountaineers really, and two of us went to climb the Breithorn on skis.

We had always considered that 1 a.m. was a critical time of day for mountaineering. We were either just coming out of the pub at 1 a.m. or else we were just crossing a bergschrund to start a big route. Once, we had left a pub in Zermatt at 1 a.m., and I had packed a sack with a minimum of gear (but including several batteries, because head torch batteries only lasted about one and a half hours those days) and set off up the hill. I had been on my own, because my brother had suddenly decided to stop climbing altogether, and I guess I had been a bit pissed off. I'd passed the hut at about 4 a.m., just as the early birds were coming out and I'd wandered up to the Breithorn and just soloed the north face, fairly briskly; no big deal, really.

So I thought the ordinary route should be easy enough to do in winter, on skis. We were on nasty hired downhill boots and poxy hired skis with rigid downhill bindings, so we just sort of side-stepped diagonally all the way up. We had no rope, no axes, no skins, no gear and no idea. All we had were shredded feet. The descent was a case of cross your fingers and tumble across those 'slot' things that you get on glaciers.

So after that we went and got the proper ski-touring gear with old-fashioned skins. They were held on with a clip at the front and straps around the ski in front of and behind the binding. Then an over-centre clip was meant to tension them up at the back. There was usually an inch of lumpy snow between the ski and the skin, so it was often a bit like skinning up a ploughed field. Then we usually had to patch them up a bit by stitching in pieces of bristly material.

So then we went to ski a proper mountain – Cross Fell, the highest point of the Pennines. The descent this time was even more difficult. No crevasses this time – just blizzards, icy rocks, frozen heather and lots of dead sheep.

Then it was the classic Haute Route from Chamonix all the way to Saas-Fee, all in terrible weather. We never saw a thing. It was fresh tracks all the way, in deep snow, but we'd climbed in Scottish winters so we could navigate a bit in nil visibility. We left one winter hut after a few days of snow in a total whiteout and some very impressed Swiss skiers followed us. I was leading our team around a spur into a bowl that dropped down towards an icefall, when there was a sudden *whoomph*. Just a little *whoomph*, but nevertheless in our ignorance, still a bit scary. I insisted that the four of us rope up, carry skis and crampon straight down the crest of the spur, all completely instinctively. The following Swiss could all ski properly, of course, so with a little guffaw at us, they jumped into the fresh powder; and the whole lot went, with a much bigger *whoomph*. There must have been a little layer of air or ice crystals in the snow pack underneath the surface. We carried on climbing straight down, and dug them out at the bottom. They lost most of their gear down the icefall but still had at least one ski each, and then they went and left me behind down the next valley, skiing on one leg. I learnt a lot that day.

As they say, the more you practise, the luckier and better you get; so by the snowy winters of the 1970s I was carrying skis up Helvellyn, for example, and skiing lots of exciting lines down Great Gully and the gullies and chimneys on the east face, sometimes jostling with climbers coming up.

I had an idea fairly early on that you could ski on a single wide ski with a lot of practice; so I made a board from marine plywood with a substantial side cut and steamed a curved prow up at the front. Then I screwed tiny steel edges to it, like some of the junior skis they sell now for youngsters. It worked in local fields so I took it up to Cairngorm. The first couple of turns on the *White Lady* actually worked, but the next one didn't. I caught a rock and one of the 'side by side' bindings ripped off. The plywood contraption went hurtling down the slope smashing out piste markers … I skulked away with the locals fuming.

Then in the 1970s some surfer in America built better single skis and so I started to ski more and more on a single monoski, with parallel bindings. It was not only great fun, but also very elegant and stylish. So, working back in the north-east, I started to monoski lots of things in the north Pennines and again in the Lake District, with the east face of Helvellyn being a favourite.

In the 1980s I broke my pelvis quite badly and for a couple of years I couldn't actually bear my body weight on my right leg. I couldn't even stand up on two normal skis. So I strapped my knackered right leg up solid in the bent-knee position, to try and support my weight, and clipped into my monoski. I couldn't press on the right leg so could only turn left, then straight and then left again, using just the one edge. Family, friends and mates were all going skiing but it was impossible to keep up. However, after a few years and lots of physio and practice I eventually got a little bit competent again and finished up doing all the big alpine runs, and more or less everything for a while, on a single ski.

Once, after skiing a peak in the Alps, I got caught in very thick cloud while descending an unfamiliar glacier, on my own. I knew there were big crevasses and ice cliff drop-offs all around, but it was as black as a bag, and I couldn't see anything. I put skins on my skis and snowploughed down really slowly. Then I rolled snowballs down in front of me, looking for holes. Then I dragged my rucksack with crampons strapped on the outside, on the end of the rope to slow me down – not that it would have stopped me going into a crevasse. In the end I got down below the clouds, still in one piece, thankfully.

After a ski trip in Chamonix with friends, when conditions were really good, I drove straight back out the next weekend on my own for a bit of an adventure. I skinned up to the bergschrund under the north-east slope of the Courtes. I stuck my skis in and self-belayed to them while climbing up on to the face, with crampons and two axes. You then pull the skis up behind and tie them on to your sack. Ski conditions are excellent when it takes two or three crampon kicks to make a good foothold. Then as the snow softens during the day as you get higher, the surface becomes nice and bitey for the ski edges, but without being so lumpy as to trip you up. As with soloing, some folk will now take big risks to be famous. The north-east slope of the Courtes is exactly forty-five degrees for 1,000 metres. On that occasion, I didn't go right to the top because it was too icy for me near the summit, but it's still a bit of a 'gripper', getting crampons off and into ski mode and calming your heartbeat, ready for that crucial first turn. Now we're skiing fifty-degree slopes that we had to cut steps up to climb when I was a youth.

During the winter of 2016, I got a bit carried away one day. I was climbing up the north side of the Petite Aiguille Verte, which is a little peak below the main Aiguille Verte and above the Grand Montets ski lift system. I was skinning up the lower slopes, which are only thirty-five degrees, and then kicking steps up soft snow on the upper slope, which is about fifty degrees. I had skis strapped to my sack, intending to ski the little face from just below the summit rocks, which I'd done many times over the previous thirty years. Then two young Swedish lads came tearing up behind in my steps, passed me, and went up to the summit snow ridge, which is like a half moon. They were going to ski the Chevalier Couloir, which is the east face of the mountain. They must have had the illusion that I was thirty years younger than I am because they kept inviting me to join them!

Anselme Baud's guidebook, which is the gospel for steep skiing, says the couloir is 'Sustained and the top section can be more than fifty-five degrees – and you use a rope to start'. So we chopped down the big cornice and looked down, and I thought it looked absolutely outrageous. I assumed these guys would drop a rope down and abseil into it, but it turned out that they were modern superstars that had skied the north face of the Aiguille du Midi under the 1,200-metre cable car. Anyone who has ever been to Chamonix will know that skiing the north face of the Midi is not for ordinary mortals; it's just for superstars – and crackpots. So these two guys clipped into their skis and just sort of dropped in. I nearly had a fit. Then they skied down, passing each other and making video films.

Fifty-five-degree snow through rocks is way too exciting for me on skis nowadays. In fact, it always was. So I cramponed down for a bit with two ice axes, until it relented to an old man's angle. Then I chopped out a ledge in the snow to get my crampons off and skis on, and then skied it from there. Even then, there was a triple bergschrund to cross at the bottom and that needed some very precise turns to negotiate, and a bit of a jump. Then it was just 2,100 metres more vertical down the glacier and pistes to the valley, relief and a brew.

Overcommitment when you're young comes from boldness and leads to innovation, development, exploration, expansion and progress. Overcommitment when you're really old comes from stupidity. I think it's time to back off a bit now; I'm seventy-five years old, for goodness sake!

The quarrying business.

Chapter 8
BUSINESS

My mother was a bit of an unrealistic soul. She wanted a lawyer, a vicar and a doctor as her three sons, but the nearest she got to that was me, the middle one, singing in Durham Cathedral as a choirboy. But I soon got out of that. I passed the maths and English exams, and also the music and singing tests, but I probably got a great big fat zero and failed the scripture exam. Otherwise I'd have been locked away like a monk in the choristers' boarding school, when all I wanted to do was ride my bike, play rugby and go climbing. What she did get eventually was a mining engineer, a civil-structural engineer and an automotive engineer: three degrees.

Initially, as a young civil engineer, I worked on a nuclear power station where we were commissioning a great big boiler house. When the two-metre diameter steam pipes heated up, they expanded sideways where they went through holes in a metre-thick reinforced concrete wall. We had to work for two days and nights continuously over Christmas to cut bigger holes through the concrete wall, and we did this by melting the steel-reinforced concrete. Yes! Melting it.

Rock and concrete melt at about 1,200 °C and this temperature can be reached by blowing oxygen and acetylene though steel tubes stuffed inside with welding rods, and then igniting it. Not surprisingly, this whole thing acts like a big flaming lance and gives off a whole lot of heat. The lance burns away very quickly, but the concrete and steel reinforcement melt and run out as red-hot molten lava. Just like a man-made volcano. Job done.

I eventually got to be a bit of an expert at renovation, restoration and strengthening of ancient, multiple-span, circular-arch masonry bridges. There are thousands of them in Britain from the northern tip of Scotland down to the southern coast of Cornwall, usually over rivers and tidal estuaries. Lots of them are damaged through modern overloading, and some are 1,000 years old. I believe that old structures have to be restored and preserved.

I've rock climbed a great deal on the limestone cliffs around the Mediterranean coast and also on our English Channel coast, and at places like Portland you sometimes see huge ammonite fossils hundreds of metres above present sea level. So it is obvious to anyone that over millions of years the sea levels have gone up and down and that land levels have altered. It's due to the Antarctic and Arctic ice masses freezing and thawing.

Magnetic variation, between magnetic north and true north, was about eight degrees when we were young, and now it's only about one degree in northern England. Two hundred and fifty million years ago, during the Permian geological age, it was very different, because at that time the equator ran around north England and since then the world has tilted. There have been barrier reefs off the north-east coast, and there have been desert conditions, eroding dry sandstones and laying down sand dunes in the direction of the then prevailing winds.

This was long before the land dropped, or the sea rose up, and a lot of Europe became covered in marine deposits forming the limestone. This silica dioxide sand underneath the limestone is very fine but has coarse grains and is ideal for making glass or mixing with cement to make mortar for bricklaying. Just after the war in the north-east everyone lived in little back-to-back terrace houses in coal pit villages. But everyone wanted better houses and so the country started to build 300,000 new houses a year in Britain, and we needed the materials to do it.

Later, my brothers and I had got sight of some National Coal Board geological maps of north-east England. We had already known that there were silica sand deposits under the sedimentary limestone and that in some places it was near the surface, far above the coal seam deposits. So in 1967, we three brothers, each with different skills, borrowed £1,000 each from the bank and paid a deposit to buy a 'tuppence-ha'penny' existing operation that was digging this sand out of a hillside and shovelling it on to builders' trucks. We rented the surface land from the county council and paid a royalty of six old pence a tonne to the church commissioners who owned the minerals – probably because Henry VIII gave the minerals to the church in exchange for a divorce. When the sand deposit got to be a bit too coarse we modified a bit of a mechanical screening plant to improve the product, and when sales increased we bought a clapped-out old loading machine, second hand, and rebuilt it. When the limestone beds above our building sand got to be too thick we improvised a rock-crashing machine to smash it into small pieces and sold that as foundation 'hardcore' for houses, factories and roads.

To start with we tried to hang on to existing jobs; but then part time became full time, and then that became extra time. After a few years we opened another quarry making a different building material, increased our mechanisation and expanded. Through the 1970s and 1980s we were operating five different quarrying companies making building sand, concreting sands and concreting aggregates, road-stone material, agricultural lime for spreading on farmland to neutralise the pH value of the soil to make potatoes and wheat grow better, and other stuff. We were operating lots of big Caterpillar machines and renting them out to competing companies when we had them spare so we could see what their operations were doing. Poor man's industrial spying if you like.

In 1970 we started going to auctions and buying bits of agricultural land when we had some spare capital, and linking those bits together into working farms. We operated partnerships for the valuable farmland, mineral leases and construction machines and ran all day-to-day production as small limited companies. We could undercut the sales prices of our big national competitors, because we had no middle management or big fancy salaries. We were partners, shareholders, directors, managers, foremen, sales reps, accountants, general dogsbodies and anything else that was required. We could set up crushing and screening plants cheaper than the competition. A big international competitor made fine agricultural lime (magnesium carbonate) by grinding magnesium limestone in very expensive electric mills. We had modified screening plants to make it cheaper. Okay, the modifications required extra vibration from oversized eccentric cams, and they broke after six months of continuous use; but we could work hard and replace them cheaply.

Some days we would sell 1,000 tonnes of building sand, 1,000 tons of concreting materials, 2,000 tons of road-stone materials when we were building the motorways, and on special days 5,000 tons of agricultural lime, exported in boats to Holland and Germany. There was one housebuilding company that was always six or eight months late in paying their suppliers' bills and they owed us quite a lot of money, which is very difficult for small private companies. So I went to one of their building sites and said to their employer, 'Does your boss pay you guys regularly? Because he certainly doesn't pay his suppliers'. He rang me up and told me to stop spreading rumours about him going broke and threatening his blokes.

I said I'd stop spreading rumours when he started paying his bills on time. Funnily enough, after that he settled our invoices regularly, every month. It's a tough life out there.

I don't want to go on about company law or partnership taxation or business things generally, but I will say that you need the right idea and equipment to make the right products at the right costs. Then you need to sell them to the right customers at the right time and at the right price. If any of these steps are wrong, then you're stuffed, lose your shirt, and go broke. Governments don't bail out private companies that make bad decisions with taxpayers' money like they do for public organisations: it's stressful and hard work and you tend to take risks. Footballers risk broken legs to earn a hundred grand a week and so would any climber – we all would.

Anyway, you're prepared to take risks and maybe a few shortcuts as well. I admit that we took a few shortcuts. Some people may have needed a paper clip across a thirteen-amp electric fuse, but I doubt if they've ever used a six-inch nail across a 350-amp cartridge fuse on a big three-phase, 450-volt power line in order to keep production going in a whole quarry. Also, we never hired a crane. If we needed to install a heavy motor or piece of equipment high up, we would rig up steel beams from excavators and loading shovels with hoist systems, and do it ourselves. After all, we were all climbers. I could rig up any kind of contraption for working at heights.

Regarding solving problems generally in life, I believe that the same principles apply to everything. You cannot solve a problem until you fully understand what the problem is. You have to stay calm, logical and analytical. For example, if your car breaks down someone has to work out which bit isn't working properly and then how to fix it. If it's a question of finance or personal money problems you need to consider where the main problem is: whether it's not enough cash coming in or too much going out. Then you need to do something about it. You cannot borrow your way out of debt. It's the same in the mountains. If you are lost and don't know where you're going, you're unlikely to find the correct route by guesswork or accident. Stop. Use what information you can gather. Work out where you are and then make the correct navigational decisions. If you are rock climbing and can't make a move, consider why: is a foot slipping on a hold, or are fingers too weak to pull on a hold? Then consider alternative solutions to doing the move. It should all be instinctive really. It's all the same in life. You'll never find the best solution to a problem until you've worked out and understood exactly what the true problem is.

We only had a few days off work each year, and I'm afraid that that was pretty damaging to domestic and family relationships. My older brother stopped climbing after we did things on the Brenva Face of Mont Blanc in about 1968 and then he just worked seven days of every week, every year. He spent his time plotting and scheming, mainly about how he could acquire his other brothers' shares. Maybe that's a bit harsh, but maybe not.

My younger brother wasn't really a rock climber, although I had managed to get him up *Diagonal* in Llanberis Pass. Then one Sunday morning we got up at 5 a.m. and blasted from Durham to the Lake District and went up Scafell. We climbed *Ichabod* and then ran down to Seathwaite and drove back to Durham for Sunday lunch at my mother's for 3 p.m. Then there was a phone call from work with a problem. The quarrying plant was malfunctioning, and I had a 5,000-tonne agricultural lime order to go on a ship for export the next day. We went straight away and worked 24 hours continuously – this was pretty much typical of those years.

In the late 1970s, we went to an auction and bought a big Georgian estate, with grand houses and farms, a deer park, woods, stables, a five-acre walled garden and the local cricket field. It all cost us less than one good family house would cost now.

One technique we used for purchases was to bid '£1,000 more than your next best offer.' Estate agents sometimes said this was illegal or that they wouldn't accept this, but probably they were being retained with backhanders by some developer. But it is legal, and I've always made sure that the seller is getting the best price possible, bypassing the agent if necessary. If the price gets too high you can always back out, but the trick always works, even for private houses when there's a closed bidding system, and I've used it several times.

But not everything went smoothly. We had quite a few thefts. One Monday morning there was no electric power to one of the quarries. Thieves had dug up a huge power cable. Someone must have stood on a rubber mat in rubber boots wearing rubber gloves and used a felling axe with a rubber handle because they had chopped through a 440-volt live cable. That's bolder than any climber I know. They'd dragged it out of a trench with a Land Rover, chopped off the other end, burnt off the insulation in a diesel-oil fire and pinched half a tonne of pure copper. They would have then weighed it in for scrap value.

On another occasion a quarry gate had been smashed down and enormous garage doors were flattened. A forty-tonne dumper truck with eight-foot-diameter wheels was missing. When the police found it, the wheels were in the ditches on opposite sides of a narrow lane, having smashed the fences on both sides. Dusty footprints on the driving seat were children's size three. A brother and sister aged eleven and twelve had squeezed through a gap in the garage doors and climbed up the ladder into the cab. There was no key. They had just pressed a button, any old button, which just happened to be the starter, and off it must have gone, automatically. There's no way they could have reached the brakes and no way they could have stopped it. It must have taken them for a terrifying ride, smashed through the locked doors, through the locked gates, down a main road at night with no lights and finally along a narrow lane into the ditches. It would just be ticking over in automatic but must have crashed and stalled.

Another theft about that time was really serious, and a case for the Special Branch. Commercial explosives for use in quarries are naturally subject to strict licences and very careful usage. They are stored in special steel cabins that are wood-lined to avoid sparks and with high security double locks. They are completely safe and can even be burnt harmlessly on a fire because they have to be 'set off' using electrical detonators, which are tiny copper cylinders connected to two long electric wires. These detonators can have various millisecond delays to make blasting more efficient and environmentally friendly. Again, they are difficult to purchase, need strict licences, come in multiple packs and are stored in a small, steel container, welded securely to the main steel cabin. This box is also wood-lined to avoid sparks and has two, high-security locks. Back in the 1970s these detonators were in great demand by certain Irish gentlemen. You wouldn't break into these steel boxes using oxyacetylene burners unless you were crackers, and rechargeable battery-powered angle grinders hadn't yet been invented. So you needed a degree in burglary to steal them. Someone had endeavoured to hacksaw a small notch across one corner of the steel box and levered open a little triangle. They'd chiselled out the wood-lining and then a very tiny hand had got inside the triangular hole. Several dozen detonators had been stolen and when the Special Branch experts come they said that two quarries in northern England had been targeted on the same weekend, using the same cunning technique.

Another explosives incident at about that time was a bit more amusing.

A farming friend said he needed to get rid of a big dead tree, but he'd been quoted £100 for a JCB for one day to dig it out, and he wasn't going to pay that. I had a licence for buying, carrying and using industrial explosives so I told him jokingly how to mix up a bag of his ammonium nitrate fertiliser with exactly four and a half pints of red tractor diesel oil to make it into ammonium nitrite and pour it into a few holes around the tree roots. I told him how to make a detonator fuel from sugar and bleach and some basic household products. I was very honourable with him, though, and warned him that if he did actually try it, he'd better stand well back. The next Saturday night he stormed up to me in the pub and fumed that it had cost him £300 to hire a JCB for three days, to fill the bleedin' hole in.

In the cold winter of 1980 I was thawing out a frozen diesel tank that probably had a bit of frozen water in the bottom of it, and doing it the quick way. It doesn't matter about the details, but the quick way involved a naked flame. The scientists will tell you that Sod's Third Law of Thermodynamics says that 'Anything that can go wrong will go wrong'. I got seriously distracted during the process and it didn't go well. It's all about the Laws of Unintended Consequences. Fortunately, my boys Martin and Simon were nearby and they both very cleverly rolled me in the snow and put me out, and it got them on to the front pages of the tabloids as nine- and ten-year-old heroes. I was very lucky that they were there, stayed calm and competent and saved me. Martin went on to become an electronics engineer and musician and Simon became an automotive engineer and climber. But I was still a bit of a mess and burnt off all my hair and a lot of skin. The specialist burns nurses said I would be in for six months and need lots of extensive skin grafts to my back and legs, but fortunately, they had just invented a burns cream made out of silver sulphonamide for coal miners who had been in a recent Glasgow coal pit explosion. There were large flaps of skin hanging off the palms of my hands and you could see black charred ligaments and bones inside. The burns nurses were brilliant and the silver cream was absolute magic. They plastered the cream inside the flaps of my hands, slapped the flaps back in, and smeared this very, very expensive silver stuff all over me with paraffin gauze dressings and wrapped me up in plastic bags. I was out of hospital in a few weeks and going to a fancy dress New Year's Eve party dressed as an invalid, but with all the genuine bandages, scabs and scars. Somebody poked me in the face saying 'Wow! That's really good make-up!'

But then things got more serious. My younger brother had his first heart attack, at only thirty-seven years old. He somehow drove his Lotus to the doctor who said he'd get the ambulance, but instead he drove himself straight into intensive care. I visited him within an hour and the big red light above his bed was flashing 210 beats per minute. He was eventually diagnosed with a rare genetic defect called Marfan syndrome, which has only recently been understood. It affects very tall thin people whose ancestors had lived in radioactive granite areas – in this case Aberdeenshire – and causes problems with the elasticity of the blood vessels. His main aorta artery out of the heart was about to burst. Fortunately, they had just started to make artificial ones out of Gore-Tex in America, but there was a problem even there. We had often ordered spare parts for big earth-moving machinery from America by Terex and we joked together that they would probably send the wrong part number from the spare-part catalogue. The surgeons opened up his chest, opened the artificial aorta package and then had to close up his chest temporarily. The artificial replacement one was only twenty-five millimetres in diameter and he needed a bigger one.

His artificial replacement was only the fourth experimental one done in the world, and afterwards I was sitting with him in intensive recovery when everything suddenly burst and blood splattered up the walls. The nurses pushed me off my chair as they shoved his bed through the crash doors back into surgery. Eventually, after forty pints of blood, they stopped the bleeding using nine swabs stuffed around the fragile stitching of the artificial graft. Eleven years later, after another heart attack, they did a scan and could read on the screen the name 'Johnson & Johnson' on some wrappers. They'd shoved the swabs in so desperately fast that they hadn't had time to take off the wrapping. Although he recovered from the first operation he couldn't take the stress of running quarries and so he started to run our farming operations, but he stopped driving Lotus and Astons and just pottered about in a Fiesta van.

Then in the mid-1980s, I did something daft and fell ten metres, landing hard on to solid concrete ground, on a straight right leg. I just felt winded, but in fact I'd forced up the right side of my pelvis and split it up the middle. The pubic symphysis joint at the front of the pelvis is flexible and held together with cartilage and ligaments. I had sheared this joint so that the right side of it was one and a half inches higher than the left side, and it had sprung across, overlapping at the front by an inch and a half as well.

In hospital a few big blokes sat on me while the orthopaedic guys tried to pull my pelvis straight, but they couldn't, so they put a big pin through my right knee and put me on traction, trying to pull the right side of the pelvis back down in line. Because of the overlap they were pulling bone against bone so that didn't work either, but they kept trying. They said that they'd never experienced this sort of injury, so I guess everyone was a bit confused. The orthopaedic surgeon went on holiday leaving the instruction 'Put as much weight on the traction as the patient can bear.' I tried to explain that I had a degree in structural engineering and understood the maths of spherical pressure vessels; but I was told to 'shut up' as I was just the 'guinea pig,' sorry, I mean the 'patient'. His deputy was apparently ex-army, so he put even more weight on. Then he went off sick and the cleaning lady put some more weights on. Eventually the big stainless-steel pin through my knee was bent into a horseshoe shape and they had my feet half a metre higher than my head to stop me being pulled out of the bed. The weights were now from the ceiling right down to the floor. After several weeks of living just on soup and ice cream I needed to go to the loo, but I was tied to this bed and couldn't move. Eventually I did a one arm pull-up on the handle above the bed that by then had a cardboard parrot nesting on it, reached to the horseshoe through my knee, untied the traction string and tied it off on the side frame of the bed. I was at last free and thought I'd go to the bathroom, but of course I just collapsed flat on the floor. It took me two hours to snake across the floor, do the necessary, crawl back and struggle back into bed, without the use of legs. When I eventually tied the weights back to the pin, the shock load nearly pulled my leg off and the scream practically woke up several patients in the morgue. Next morning a coal miner in the next bed with a broken back said to my wife, 'Hey Missus! He was out of bed in the night!' She said 'Don't talk daft. He can't move.'

After a few weeks another doctor came into my room, saw my traction and said 'Gawd! What on earth are we doing to this patient – I don't care where he is – get these weights off – two or three pounds each day … ' In the end a nurse admitted quietly that they should have only had about one-pound weight of traction per stone of body weight; that is about twelve pounds, instead of nearly 40 pounds. I asked another nurse if I'd ever climb 6b rock climbs and she said 'Yeah! No problem'. I said 'Well, that's just great, because I couldn't before I came in!'

When the weights were finally off and they realised they couldn't straighten me out and realign the pelvis, they said I could go home as soon as I could master the stairs on crutches. So naturally I got crutches that same day and went head over heels down the stairs. Literally – the stairs had just been washed and mopped and were lethal. The exact discharge words were: 'Forget about running and skiing. You'll never climb again. You won't be able to walk normally. And you'll probably be in a wheelchair in five years' time.' Frightening!

I struggled for six months trying to shuffle around on crutches, with pelvis bones scraping together and grinding and clicking. By then my right leg was just a thin bone with a big, fat, swollen knee. I had a sequence of eighteen X-rays taken, and the final one eventually showed a bit of calcification across the joint, as the supposed flexible joint in my pelvis started to set but still twisted three centimetres out of line. I was then referred back into a warm physio pool to move around a bit with some injured coal miners, to try and build up some new leg muscle. After three years of physiotherapy three times a week, I eventually built up one short fat thigh muscle and the other one long and thin, but with the pelvis and backbone still badly twisted and curved.

During this period there was no way that I could rush about and work the way we had done. With my younger brother struggling with his health, by the late 1980s we three brothers were falling apart with different ideas and ambitions. Older brother tried to confiscate young brother's company shares because he had no children, and then give them to his own four children. He tried to assimilate our valuable partnership assets into his own company, to manipulate accountants, and lots of other stuff. I could write a whole book on company and partnership law, on fiddles and manipulations and really dirty tricks. Needless to say it all got out of hand, we all fell out, and it became terminal.

My younger brother who was seriously ill and I – who could barely shuffle about – wanted to split away from our elder, ruthless brother, who was the only one now fit enough to work seven days a week. Big brother was continually trying to get two thirds majority votes over minority one thirds, and everything became more and more nasty. Big debts were taken on and exaggerated in order to hide or reduce the value of other assets.

During the 1960s, 1970s and early 1980s we had been working like crazy and buying bits of farmland at auctions whenever we made a bit of profit. We were continually opening new quarries and making new building material products. It came to a head one day in the 1980s when we were chatting to banking people about finance, overdrafts, bankruptcy and such everyday matters, as you do. Anyway, after much manoeuvring, this eventually led to a big meeting with auditors, solicitors and accountants and us. I think we had twenty-eight different meetings in quick succession all in one day. There were directors' meetings, shareholders' meetings and partnership meetings for three different partnerships and six different limited companies that we had started, and everything was split up. But because of our different health problems, it wasn't done in a particularly equitable way.

I suppose the bottom line was that Father, before he died, supported his eldest son. Mother was able to move to a comfortable little bungalow and try to forget the hassle there had been in the family. Older brother got what he wanted and had worked so hard to get, which was the Georgian estate and quarry business and valuable mineral leases. Younger brother was happy to potter about and run our farms while hanging on to his remaining health. The outcome for me was that I withdrew from the quarrying business. My priority was to learn to walk again and try to get back some mobility. I spent a few years hobbling about and slowly my body learnt to cope with the new geometry of my twisted pelvis, without the pressures of the previous workload.

The stress of private business and working long hours had put strains on families and relationships, and as we know, few things last forever. In the 1980s I married my new wife Sylvie who helped me through my years of injury and we are still together, all of the time. I believe that there are very few other people in the whole world that are the right partner for any one person, with the right character, personality, interests, background, attitudes, looks, etc. If you are lucky enough to find that one person, then you are indeed very lucky: a good soul mate is for life.

Together with my second wife Sylvie, I inherited a splendid stepdaughter, Kate, who is very successful. She is now a partner in a law firm and specialises in corporate litigation. That's Latin for 'sues naughty businessmen'. Anyway, the moral of all this family and business stuff is, in my opinion, to trust your chosen friends rather than the people imposed upon you by blood.

Guiding in the Alps. © Peter Allison Collection

Chapter 9
GUIDING

The traction weights loaded on to the pin just below my knee had been so excessive that they had stretched the knee ligaments and pulled my knee apart. That, together with the constant grafting and clicking of the pelvis bones while hobbling about on crutches, had made any kind of physiotherapy very difficult. But after a couple of years of gentle movement I started to build up a bit of strength in my legs again. The different shape of my thigh muscles and the twisted healing of the pelvis meant that my backbone now had a curve in it, but at least I was slowly recovering from what the medics said would be a 'wheelchair future'.

So, after about three years, I started hitting the physiotherapy gym and, in particular, the step machine – in my head and with my eyes closed, kicking steps up an alpine north face. That positive attitude definitely aided my recovery. After lots of sessions, with sweat dripping from me, I was doing the equivalent of 1,000 metres of uphill in an hour or two. So they kicked me out and I felt ready to get back on the hill again.

In the late 1980s, Sylvie and I were staying with some good friends in their chalet down the valley below Arolla in Switzerland. I had climbed and skied the Pigne d'Arolla a few times in the past because it has a gentle glacier on the south side right up to the summit. But I'd always been attracted to the north face, which is one of the easiest of the classic north faces. I'd not read any guidebook, but I'd always spied a good line that looked skiable, not too technical: just get up a gully on to a higher glacier, around a few ice séracs and up the top 300-metre snow slope at about forty-five degrees or so, to the summit.

Arolla village is at 2,000 metres and the summit is about 3,800 metres. So I left Arolla at 2 a.m. one morning in spring with head torch, water bottle, duvet jacket and my two-metre Rossignol monoski tied to my rucksack and walked up beside the closed drag lift and then up the glacier to a biggish crevasse at the foot of the north side. It was a bit precarious getting across some snow bridges unroped and then around the side of some steeper sections. Then there was nice snow up through some séracs and an easy crampon romp up the top slopes to the summit, by about 9 a.m. The first turns off the summit on a monoboard were quite intimidating, with several thousand metres of exposure down to the valley. One thousand eight hundred metres of vertical.

A couple of hours later I was showered, changed into normal clothes, sitting around a dining table, eating a formal lunch, with polite conversation with normal people, and my mind wandered … Hours earlier I had been on my own on a big face, depending on crampon points and then on a single ski edge – on a different planet really. I recalled that on previous occasions I had spent four nights tied to little ledges, and seven whole days on three separate occasions on the North Face of the Eiger. And yet now here I was again, with normal people trying to be 'normal and ordinary'.

I sometimes think I have two different personas, existing and performing on two different planes, one vertical and one horizontal. I have always felt comfortable and relaxed on a steep mountainside. I believe that we are all programmed into our own personal genetic history.

My ancestors must have lived for thousands of years wandering the fells and hills of northern Britain, over snow and icy rocks. They would be building homes from stone and wooden furniture, digging up peat, smelting tools from copper and iron, living on bread baked from oats with root vegetables and rabbit, or even wild venison when they could catch it. Some people imagine that their ancestors were either 'upstairs' and posh, or 'downstairs' and servants. I think our ancestors got used to a certain way of life over hundreds of years, and the genes that we inherit prepare us for a similar environment to them. As I say, I personally have always been quite comfortable either halfway up or halfway down a steep, snowy mountainside.

So there we are: I was coming up to fifty years old and had already retired from two proper careers and was getting my health and fitness back at last. So what to do next? I remembered as a teenager climbing in the Lake District in the 1950s hearing about an old codger living in a cave in Borrowdale in the 1920s who had advertised himself as a 'Professor of Adventure, near misses almost guaranteed'. I had always thought that 'near misses definitely avoided' would have brought in more customers.

I had a desire to put something back into the climbing world, maybe to help people fulfil their mountaineering ambitions and keep them safe in what we all know is a risky environment. So I signed up for the British Mountain Guides scheme. I had thought that in the very early days it had been fairly straightforward, but by then it had become international and much more professional and demanding. The continentals had insisted that the British learnt to ski properly, and I like to think that we had helped to improve their rope-work safety. As a young lad I had seen some terrible rope handling by continental alpinists, for example, big diagonal falls on to poxy direct belays.

The assessments were very rigorous with several residential weeks of tests in rock climbing, Scottish winter climbing, alpine mountaineering, off-piste skiing, ski touring, and mountain first aid. Many good climbers fail the standards, usually due to issues about the care of clients, or a weakness in their ability to navigate accurately in the mountains at night or in bad weather. Micronavigation in a Scottish blizzard is not easy.

On assessment, I was a bit disappointed that I was asked to help a candidate who was more a mountain skier, rather than a climber, to get through a rock climbing assessment because he was of a more mature age. In fact, I was much older than him, but no one had made it easy for me. Actually, I think I was the oldest candidate in the world, at about fifty, to successfully complete and pass all the rigorous assessments of the International Federation of Mountain Guides Associations, which then was still the Union Internationale des Associations des Guides de Montagnes.

One candidate was being assessed for his personal climbing skills in winter and was leading a mixed rock and ice climb on Ben Nevis. His assessor was sitting in a snow bucket seat belayed in a snowy gully. He went up about ten metres and clipped into a little sling on a loose spike for a runner. Then he shuffled up another ten metres or so and put a little wire nut into a crack. Then he got up a bit further and got a poor cam runner into a crack between the ice and the rock. Then he eventually wobbled up a bit higher, before falling off into space. The cam pulled out. Then the nut pulled out. Then the little spike broke off and he splatted into the snowy gully down below the assessor's belay, which pulled out. As they both slid head over heels, for hundreds of metres down the easy snow gully, the candidate on assessment was heard to shout, 'I suppose that means that I've fai-ai-iled … '

Another chap was called Miles, but we called him 'Kilometre' for short. He was doing a rock climb in Llanberis Pass called *Grond*. It's an overhanging crack that you have to layback up because there are not many holds.

To layback you put hands in the crack and pull sideways, with feet on the other side in opposition, using friction. If you are strong you cruise up. If you are not you shuffle up. And if you're weak you fall off. At one time it was difficult to place runners to protect against a leader's fall, but in the 1970s some bloke invented things he called Friends. They are cam devices with springs so that they open out and jam – even in flared cracks – so a leader can clip them into the main rope and protect themselves. Anyway, they were clever bits of kit and exorbitantly expensive (they still are), so this guy only had one of them.

He laybacked up a bit and clipped into the Friend. Then he laybacked up a bit higher, reached down and took the Friend out from below and replaced it up above his head. Then he went up a bit more reached down and again repositioned his single friend up above his head again; his only runner jammed securely in the crack. When he was about ten metres up the climb and repeating this process for about the fourth time he suddenly fell off. Unfortunately, he'd got his timing wrong. In fact he'd got everything wrong. His strength, the friction, his nerve, everything. As he hit the deck he still had his Friend in his outstretched hand above his head.

As an example of the types of assessments in the guides' scheme, you may have to simulate all kinds of scenarios. Splint a pretend broken arm while hanging from slings halfway up a rock climb. Abseil a stretcher down a steep climb. Abseil with a casualty past an 'accidental' knot in the abseil rope. Count paces on a compass bearing while navigating at night in bad visibility. Crevasse rescue hoists with a minimum of gear and lots of other simulated, tricky problems, all of which can and do happen while looking after clients or less experienced people in the mountains.

I once had to pull someone out of a big crevasse on my own. Their crampons had 'balled' up – that is, soft afternoon snow had stuck to the crampons on a descent forming a ball so that the points wouldn't stick into the snow. This person had slid down steep, soft snow for six metres and plopped into a crevasse about five metres down and was hanging from a rope wearing a climbing harness. Fortunately, it was an easy matter to drop a spare loop of rope and do a simple three-in-one hoist. Most qualified mountain guides will have practised this a lot, been assessed doing it and probably had to do it for real a few times.

A professional guide has to be continuously thinking one step ahead, about what could possibly go wrong, and be ready to improvise and deal with absolutely any eventuality. I was, however, involved in a rather questionable situation. I was being assessed for personal winter climbing competence by an examiner with a reputation for being difficult with amateur mountaineers, who maybe had a positive reputation for their climbing expertise and experience, but who, like me, had no instructing experience in an outdoor school.

At the top of a technical climb he asked to look at one of my crampons; but he took it and put it in his rucksack, as much as to say 'Now! What you going to do?' I thought, 'Okay! Two can play at that game of snakes'. I suggested that he could take one of his off as well, if he liked. He must have thought it would be okay, because I would have to cut steps up to the summit and he would be on a top rope anyway so I said, 'Okay! I'm not being assessed for looking after a client, I'm being assessed for personal climbing skills.' I unclipped the rope, and nicked a few little footsteps for one uncramponed boot as I had done loads of times as a youth, and soloed up to the summit. I don't think he was well pleased.

However, all that aside, it's a very difficult qualification to get, and everyone I know is hugely proud to be allowed to wear the International Guides badge.

After I retired from proper work, we moved to live in an old church that my wife Sylvie and I converted, near the coast in Snowdonia. When we had restored and converted an old smallholding in the national park of North Yorkshire, the building had been shown on county maps of 350 years ago. We made a cow byre into a sitting room, a forge into a kitchen and a pigsty into a granny flat, but there had been seven pages of planning conditions, regarding roof construction, type of stone work, window lintels and sills and window styles, etc. When we got planning to convert the church in North Wales for a domestic dwelling, it had initially been refused, but the planning officer had then been sacked and went to jail for fraud and bribery. Later when I reapplied using a more Welsh sounding surname (because you can actually apply for planning consent in anyone's name) it was passed and there was only one short sentence of planning conditions. Namely: no caravans in the grounds while doing the renovation and conversion work. At this time I already had an apartment in the Chamonix Valley and so I started to climb half the year and to ski the other half of the year and soon built up a group of good regular clients for enthusiastic mountain adventures, all around the world.

Setting up the apartment in Argentière and furnishing it was actually quite amusing. We had taken a load of English furniture out there on a big trailer behind a four-by-four truck with a personalised registration plate. Afterwards we were coming back through Dover customs in November at 3 a.m. with an empty trailer behind a rough vehicle with dodgy plates.

My alpine apprenticeship had been in the late 1950s when the road up to Chamonix was still a rough gravel cart track up the other side of the valley, long before the present roads were built. It was a single lane and some old blokes in overalls and with long-handled shovels were shovelling gravel into the potholes just in front of vans to fill the holes in. This was the only road up to Chamonix then.

I started off guiding by taking people up the good classic Alpine routes that I'd already done as an amateur. The Chamonix Aiguilles; the Aiguille du Chardonnet; Aiguille d'Argentière; Gervasutti Couloir; Gervasutti Pillar; routes on the Aiguille du Midi, and then the bigger things on the Grandes Jorasses, Mont Blanc and all over Switzerland.

Then there's the Matterhorn, probably the most recognised mountain in the world, on the front of all those boxes of chocolates, and it's horribly overcrowded. On a day of good weather, which means a bad day of congestion, there can be fifty climbers making the ascent and there's not much room for passing in many places. It's as bad as Snowdon or Great Gable or Everest.

If your ambition is to climb the Matterhorn then you'd better do it soon, because it's loose and it's falling down and it might not be there by next year. On the Hörnli Ridge you've got to short-rope and climb together. If you set out to pitch it and belay you'll be stuffed and take forever. The route follows little ledges and gullies and ribs and slabs. Don't follow the tiny cairns that the Swiss guides have built to confuse you. Follow the tiny luminous pen marks in pink or yellow that show up in your head torch. If you spot these short cuts you might pass a few folk each time. If you do it in a brisk three and a half hours or a slow six hours it will always take you a quarter of an hour longer to come back down safely. And I'll bet you ten quid on that one.

One Belgian client had climbed with me so much that he could second grade V on pure ice climbs. On the *Frendo Spur*, in perfect conditions, we climbed all the top ice pitches together short roping, because we had great trust in each other. I guided the *Frendo Spur* and north face of the Aiguille du Plan so many times that I built little stone bungalows, without planning permission, around boulders at suitable bivvy sites. It was much better for clients to take two half-days to experience such routes rather than one big day, and to get the top ice slopes in better condition early next morning.

We had originally done rock routes on the south face of the Midi in big curly boots carrying big sacks with primus stoves and steel billycans, pulling on pegs and slings. But now we could guide big rock routes in rock shoes carrying only chalk bags and water. I've even gone down the Midi ridge in trainers.

Once we bivvied in the Midi cable station to go for a route early on Mont Blanc du Tacul, but there was a wind in the night. It was draughty there in the old days, so we got inside the little old cabin, before it was modernised and rebuilt. At 2 a.m. I realised that they'd moved the 'bin' out of the station by a few metres in the night, because of the wind. We had to put the ropes around the central pole and abseil down on to steep ice, in the dark. A good start to a route, and a good lesson in abseiling for anybody.

Regarding the ski-touring side of guiding, it's all about the gear working properly. Skins coming off, bindings breaking, people nervously carrying too much gear, and sometimes not enough. With new touring clients I sometimes tip their sacks out to check their gear, because a small problem in the mountains soon leads to a big one, and a big problem sometimes turns into an epic.

Once in a hut in the eastern Alps, there was a big group of elderly Austrians using ancient touring bindings. The frame swivelled up on a pin through the front of the ski, but unfortunately most of the pins had worn through and broken. Fortunately, there was an iron poker in this winter hut that was just the right diameter, and I always carried a bit of broken backsaw blade in my tool kit. We cut the poker into short pieces, tapped them into place with a rock, and riveted the ends over with an ice axe, and fixed all their binding problems. Unfortunately, I couldn't fix their snoring problems, except by throwing gear at them in the night. Next morning I had no gear left.

On another occasion the gear problem was a bit more serious. A client's touring binding pulled right out of a ski in the middle of nowhere, so we needed to drill a hole in the ski using a little percussion drill bit that I used to carry. You keep tapping it and turning it. Then we could fix the binding back on. While I was modifying my improvisations, the guy himself had a go with a Swiss Army knife, but he only managed to slip and cut the end off his finger. We suddenly had a red coloured glacier, but we managed to stop the bleeding, put the tool kit to one side so it wouldn't be lost in the deep snow, and then stick the end back on the finger with glue and stiches. When I eventually tied the binding back to the ski, he had one heel up and one heel down, but at least he managed to ski for another three days, and they all completed their tour. Even the finger healed. There were no helicopter rescues in those days. Sometimes you need a PhD in bodging gear on ski-touring trips.

Another essential skill for guiding is mountain navigation. If you can micronavigate at night, in a whiteout in the winter Cairngorms you should be okay anywhere in the world. Once, we left a hut in really thick 'clag' with several international groups, skinning up a badly crevassed glacier. First the leading group stopped for drinks and then the second group stopped, pretending that ski-skins had come off. Then the third group looked worried and lost, and suddenly we were at the front with nil visibility. I'd been up this glacier many years earlier as a young lad and had actually broken through a crevasse but was stopped because of a huge rucksack with spare ski sticks strapped across the top, and they jammed at the top. So we kept well across to the safe side. Then, over the top of the col, we had to ski down on a compass bearing to a certain altitude and then on a different bearing for a set distance to get around some ice séracs that we couldn't see but knew were there. The night before, in huts, I always write crucial navigation bearings and altitudes on the back of my hand as a crib, so I don't have to keep getting the map out. On this occasion we came down out of the cloud exactly where we should be and the other international guided groups all caught us up and gave a big round of applause. Stupid, but quite amusing really.

After we did the first British ascent of Lyskamm north face as youths, we had been staggering back down the glacier and I'd gone into a monster crevasse. We'd actually done the route not when it was nice crisp new snow, nor when it was hard frozen ice. It was nothing but deep slush. I remember kicking and stamping steps in soft stuff up to my knees, all the way up the face. I now know that it was probably all just about to avalanche off, but we didn't understand conditions when we were youths. On the descent the glacier was soft as well. At the time we had absolutely no idea about safe glacier travel or crevasse rescue. We were actually a threesome and one mate had never really worn crampons before. I was at the back and supposedly watching the others, but we were knackered and there was loads of spare rope trailing about on the glacier and I had lots of coils of rope in my hands. There was about a foot of soft snow on the surface and we all stepped, in turn, wide, over a little crack …

Suddenly I was twenty metres down a hole the size of St Paul's Cathedral, swinging free, tied to a bowline around the waist, with tight coils around my hand and blood running up my arm from a rope-burnt hand. Worse still, I was miles from either side and I was slowly dropping lower and lower as they were pulled backwards through the slush on the surface. I was spinning slowly, because that's what happened on an old hawser-laid rope. It was a big black void below, and I was still sinking.

Eventually they and their rucksacks ploughed backwards to a stop, but they had no idea how to make a belay in slush or how to do a crevasse hoist and I had even less of an idea of how to prusik out. We hadn't yet invented climbing harnesses and we weren't familiar with any kind of system for climbing up a single rope. I quickly got the weight off my chest by standing in a thin sling twisted several times around the rope, but then it took about two hours to improvise and work out a way to climb up a rope with prusik slings, back in those early years.

Emergencies, panic and fear are probably the 'mothers of invention' and eventually I crawled over the lip of the crevasse like a drowned fish, but my mates still hadn't got a decent anchor in the slush. Because of this experience, I have always been keen to run 'ski-bum' courses, teaching lots of good skiers about alpine crevasses, avalanches and a bit about mountain craft generally. Skiers in big mountains need to know about navigation, crevasse rescue, rope work, avalanche prediction and awareness, and lots of other stuff. I like to think that in two or three days I can teach the important skills safely that it has taken me fifty-odd years to learn the hard way.

Way back in the 1960s, before snow-holing became popular in the Cairngorm winters, we were slightly lost somewhere in Europe because of a bit of careless navigation, and we were caught out in a proper good winter blizzard. Even then I carried a crude aluminium shovel that I could fix to an ice axe. We were clearly going to suffer if we didn't get out of the weather quickly. So we furiously dug out a hole in the snow pack and reinforced the roof with skis and sticks. It snowed three metres in three days and we were inside the snow for all three days. Somebody kept blocking up the entrance because it was draughty, but I knew instinctively that we would suffocate, so I kept clearing it out. Not only did we survive, it was actually quite cosy and we realised that you could cope with almost any kind of weather in the mountains if only you could get into a snow hole and out of the wind. I think we even sculpted an imitation TV set in the corner, out of ice; but the reception was rubbish. The picture was just a bit snowy!

About fifty years later in a similar situation, but with clients, and now in the telecommunications age, we couldn't get a mobile phone signal, so in between sharing out the last seventeen raisins and segments of squashed orange, we made a big dish out of aluminium survival blankets and put a phone in the centre. It worked, and we got a magnified signal. There's nothing like a few tricks of the trade. It's just the same as any other activity in life, although sometimes a bit more life-threatening in the mountains.

This particular incident was probably as bad as any I've experienced in the mountains, though. We were doing a one-day ski tour in winter and we knew the weather was going to deteriorate, looking at the condition of the sky, by the following day. I had an ex-army guy with me who had snow-holed for fun in the Arctic Circle, but also a German couple who were not so bold. We had to skin up from a glacier for a couple of hours and then carry the skis up an icy gully for a bit. On the top the 'clag' came in quite quickly, but my couple didn't fancy retreating back down the gully, even with a top rope. One person's 'jolly up' is another person's epic. We had caught up with another group, so even though we were delayed a bit, we carried on. I knew the terrain and we had to traverse around the head of another glacier on skis for about half a mile. But the snow was starting to fall quite heavily, and it got more and more difficult to break trail and maintain the high traverse line. As the snow started to fall even more heavily, the visibility decreased and slowly we lost height down towards some small crevasses that I knew were there, but that we couldn't see.

As the visibility got worse I suddenly broke thought a little cornice that shouldn't have been there, and slid six metres or so down a slope into a small crevasse. Then I banged pretty hard on to an ice bridge, hurting my knee. It was easy enough to sidestep back up and out and rejoin what was now a group of ten, but by now two feet of new snow had fallen and visibility was nonexistent. We roped up and carried on skiing on a rough compass bearing, but we were in a tricky spot with nil vision and the correct decision was a snow hole for us all.

I thought we'd rest up for a few hours until it cleared and then carry on with the ski descent in the evening, in nice new powder snow. But the snowfall got heavier and it snowed all night. Hence, the improvised satellite phone dish. The next day it snowed even more heavily. The snow hole roof, which we had dug in haste the day before, was starting to collapse under the weight of new snow, so we dug a posh new one with supporting columns and barrel vaulted ceilings, two doors and seat pews for all ten people. It was a bit like a Grade II listed cathedral. But it was getting even deeper outside and very avalanchy. During the second night, the permanent ice pack on my knee was not enough and it was swelling and getting painful, so I used a snow shovel handle and a roll of duct tape to splint my leg in a bent-knee ski position. As it turns out, I found out later from X-rays that the bone was cracked and broken, just below the knee, where the traction pin had been hammered in and pulled the knee apart all those years earlier.

Then it snowed hard again all that next night. By the middle of the next day the snow eased off and although it had snowed about three metres we could actually see about thirty yards. We roped up into two groups of five and very carefully, aware of the extreme avalanche risk, started to snow-plough out and down. Everyone was absolutely fine, although some were a bit chilly and one of the other group had cold toes in thin socks and down-hill boots. I had my usual three pairs of socks, in touring boots, and went for an X-ray a few days later. It had been -28 °C outside but a balmy -1 °C inside, with a bit of a candle lit. The next night everyone went to a restaurant and had four courses of food with double chips at every course, and just a few gallons of beer. They had all survived a proper winter storm, but only by getting inside a proper snow cave. Oh, and I'd skied out with a broken leg, self-splinted.

After the 1999 avalanche in the Chamonix Valley, we were inundated by world reporters looking for a sensational story and we all decided not to speak to them. We professionals had been out all night with head torches, shovels and transmitter/receivers, digging in the debris of thousands of tonnes of avalanched snow and thirteen chalets, some that had been up-ended and moved fifty metres or more. One guy, who we now call 'Sledgehammer Mike', smashed through the cracked concrete wall of a chalet that had been upended twenty-four hours ago, and three frightened little children climbed out. But sadly thirteen people died in their homes that day. The media started to say stupid things, so we all decided that I would talk to Sky News and other colleagues would talk to the BBC and ITV.

I tried to explain to reporters and demonstrate how the 'pisteurs' and mountain guides dig pits into the snow pack and check the layers of old snow so that predictions of avalanche risk can be made. Unfortunately, the mountain doesn't know that we are supposed to be experts, so there are always some risks, but we do always try to minimise it by using the best gear and equipment. And, as ever, the more knowledge and understanding you have, the better.

Regarding off-piste ski guiding, I always used to ask my groups if they wanted to ski 'this boring red run' or did they fancy going around the corner for a bit of an adventure? Surprisingly enough, it was always the 'adventure' answer. The only way to improve is to get in there and try it, and with the right sort of help in the right conditions and environment, people improve their skiing very quickly.

With snowboarding, for example, some instructors keep novices messing about on the flat for days, but I always found that the best way was for them to carry their boards straight away up on a chair lift and then sit down on an easy run but with a decent slope to it. Strap on the board and sideslip down, facing out. After a bit, do a 'falling leaf'. Release the edge at the front, then at the back, but keep the board across the slope. It's no good talking about the 'fall line' to novices, they don't know what you mean, unless they're climbers as well. I once told a skier to stand on the outside ski on turns. After a whole week I said, 'Lift the inside ski on turns'. He thought that was much better, but didn't seem to realise it's the same thing. For the snowboarders, after a couple of goes I got them to try a 'falling leaf' but facing in, and looking where they're going over the shoulder. They're bound to have a few sit-downs and even a few head-plants occasionally, so they need a bit of padding. A towel over the hips inside the overtrousers is useful, and good support on the wrists is essential. Just a few hours are sufficient on the first couple of days. With this technique people soon learn to understand the edges and are linking turns on easy ground very quickly. Then they're boarding proper runs in just a few days. The body picks up snowboarding instinctively. It's the head that gets in the way. Just relax and let the body do it; don't try to analyse the mechanism.

I had lots of snowboarding groups for the classic Vallée Blanche, for example, and they soon want to do the big off-piste adventures with a mountain guide. Snowboarding and monoskiing and proper skiing are all completely different, but there is one common factor, and that is the proper understanding of edge control. There are two common factors: the mountain environment and the conditions, and that takes either many years of experience or else a bit of intensive instruction. With all my groups I have always insisted on about half a day per week of mountaincraft, and this involves simulating all sorts of situations. Firstly, I would always loan all skiers an avalanche 'transceiver.' Then we would traverse around a corner away from any crowds. We would consider the snowfall over the last few weeks, the wind conditions of the last few days and the temperature and aspect of slope at the moment. I would continually stab a ski stick into the snow pack and see if there were separate crusty layers. Then we would pretend or assume that there really was an avalanche risk. You use a portable shovel to dig into the snow pack and isolate a column of snow layers maybe one metre high and half a metre square. Then evaluate the hardness and wetness of the snow in each different layer, on a scale of one to five. If adjacent layers are very dissimilar then it is unlikely that the bond between the layers will be very high. Then pull the column out, with the shovel or a ski and see how easily the layers separate and slide apart. With experience you can then assess the avalanche risk on that particular slope, again on a scale of one to five. If it's high, go straight to the pub; if it's low, then pretend it's high and choose a safe line to ski. Straight down a spur is okay because the avalanche debris goes to either side, but if you have to cross a gully or a bowl then choose a feature of safety such as behind a boulder or tree and go one at a time, watching each other carefully. If the slope is really unstable then rope up and belay each other.

Then, go to the bottom of a bowl and pretend that you've been properly avalanched. I would lay out simulated debris, rucksacks and skis and jackets and a buried transceiver in a plastic bag. Then everyone in the group must learn how to locate a buried victim, quickly – lives may depend on it. There are dozens of avalanche deaths every year in the European Alps – fifty-seven in one recent winter in the Mont Blanc area alone. If you're digging out a real avalanche victim in a real situation then dig like crazy. Dig in shifts helping each other. An avalanche victim is always a medical case, and will always need treatment for something – shock at the very least. Clear the airways and get straight on to find the next victim – quickly. A qualified international mountain guide or an experienced ski tourer should be able to find half a dozen hidden transmitters very quickly in a simulated situation and everyone should practise regularly.

Assessing the avalanche risk by considering the previous wind and snow conditions and then digging and testing snow pits is sometimes just not sufficient. I think it helps to have a sort of basic instinct for it. It needs a shedload of experience in the environment. It's almost like an instinctive smell for it. Of course by the summer all the winter snow has slid down the hillside or evaporated and disappeared. The trick for ski tourers is to make sure you're not underneath it all in the spring, just as it all decides to fall down – you can have that advice for free.

In 1999, at the time of the big Chamonix-Montroc avalanche there were big avalanches throughout the European Alps. In Evolène-Arolla in Switzerland people were killed inside their chalets; the Swiss authorities thought that conditions were so dangerous that they kept reporters out of the valley. They even stopped rescuers from going anywhere near. These avalanches also happened across Austria on similar facing slopes and they were all 'powder' avalanches, which are really much more common in Canada than in Europe. These avalanches all occurred within a few days of each other as the exceptional snowstorms crossed over Europe.

Powder avalanches happen due to a huge build up of new snow that is too heavy to be supported by the bond on to the old layers below. The bond shears and the soft snow slides off, becoming airborne and moving at very high speed. Powder avalanches are not so common in Europe because we have too much wind. The wind breaks up the flakes of falling snow and blows it over ridges and cols, and dumps the granules together on the slopes in hard-packed layers that are not properly bonded on to the old layer below. This is 'windslab'; sometimes there may be only a couple of inches of windslab and it is not dangerous, but if the wind has blown in one direction for a couple of weeks, say in Scotland, the windslab can be five metres thick. If a skier cuts through it or climbers overload it, the bond between the layers will shear and separate off and big chunks come down, like huge paving slabs. The debris can be many metres deep and sets like concrete. For the unwary or unlucky, the only chance of survival is for everyone to be wired-up with transmitters/transceivers, and for everyone to know how to use them. I have known even experienced professional guides who have died because they weren't using them.

The more time you spend in the mountains, the more your personal odds are altered. I was only once in a very small avalanche, a long time ago. I was carrying the rucksack of a slightly injured companion as well as my own, so was very overloaded. As I crossed a little gully on skis, about six inches of snow broke away above me. I was carried down about six metres and instinctively rolled forward and forward, and easily rolled out of the other side. But the debris carried on down into a gorge, and these moments always leave you shocked. I know people who have been avalanched a number of times. Once is good experience. Twice is reckless. Don't ever leave the valley with anyone who's been avalanched three times. And that's more good advice.

I think everyone should at least have seen a crevasse rescue simulated, because it's difficult to understand from a book, and you need to have a bit of an idea about rope-work. I have come across a group of off-piste skiers where the leader has dropped a few feet into a crevasse and no one had a clue how to make a belay anchor, let alone how to do a hoist. I personally would never ski anywhere serious without a transceiver, shovel and thirty metres of eight-millimetre rope. If you're out with mates, make sure everyone is wired up and transmitting.

As my regular ski groups got to be better and more adventurous, I did lots of steeper ski weeks. I would use 100 metres of seven-millimetre rope and make a belay with my skis at the top of a forty-five-degree gully. Then I'd use a waist belay so that you can let out the rope quickly and safeguard their first twenty or so turns. The rope doesn't get in the way and doesn't catch the ski heels on steepish ground, but it certainly saves a few long falls. I often climbed couloirs with ski clients and kept them belayed on a rope at the top while they got crampons off and skis on, and composed themselves for those first few cautious turns. I consider this to be crucial, because at the top of one of my favourite steep runs, a Dutchman in a different guided group slipped. A ski slid away while he was trying to clip into it and he tried to grab it. He was unroped and fell a long, long way. He only slipped that once.

There are lots of steeper slopes available in the Argentière-Chamonix area for the people who want to do this type of skiing. There are stacks of stuff to do, for those that can and those that want to. The 'extreme' superstars are now skiing faces of fifty degrees and more. But I've got to say, there aren't many of them around, and often they don't get to be very old.

Then there is Couloir Philippe, a narrow gully under the bottom cable car of the Grands Montets ski system in Argentière. You sideslip down through a couple of steel avalanche barriers then put in a few turns at about forty degrees, and then ski down easily past bushes and trees. My two sons skied it with me when they were only thirteen or fourteen years old and most of my keen clients have done it regularly, although I always put them on a top rope for the top bit on their first go.

Sometimes if a person was a bit nervous on a long, steep descent I'd keep them on a short rope of six metres or so, with a few coils for slack, and let them ski one turn at a time, while I would protect them on a sideslip with edges well into the snow. It's a good thing to have an ice axe out ready as well, in this situation. And tell folks to remember to breathe. Some folk want to try it but are so tense when in extremis that they forget that they need lots of oxygen. On one occasion skiing a forty-five-degree couloir under the Dru, the conditions were a bit avalanchy, so I stuck a client's skis into the snow and belayed myself. Then I jumped on the snow pack on skis to set off the loose snow. Then we all skied the bitey, hardpack underneath, nice and safely.

Another good ski-mountaineering peak that we've done several times with clients, both summer and winter, is the north side of Mont Blanc du Tacul. It isn't particularly steep, but there are several bands of séracs to get past and quite a few crevasses. One summer it had rained heavily in the valley for three days and a few of us were considering what to do. I thought there must be good snow somewhere high up so we went up on the Aiguille du Midi with our ski gear. On the top it was cloudy, and I began to think I'd made a mistake. My good friend and colleague 'Big Nick' – who is only four-foot-eleven inches tall, but is a brilliant skier – was with me, together with others, and I was so embarrassed that we took our guides badges off. But we skied across to the Tacul and skinned up the face and then cramponed up past the tricky bits. There was a twelve-metre-wide strip of perfect new powder snow about one foot deep all the way down the middle of the face for 760 metres, filling in the crevasses and easing the angle through the sérac bands. The weather cleared and the descent was just brilliant. Being September, we couldn't carry on down the Vallée Blanche, but we were so buzzing that we actually skinned all the way back up the Midi ridge to the cable car. Then we looked through the station windows back at our tracks coming down from the summit, which I have to say were quite excellent. We bumped into a couple of French mountain guides who I knew and they gave us the thumbs up and said, 'Good one – good decision.' I was quite chuffed really: a good day for September, skiing fresh tracks in virgin powder at 4,200 metres.

I'm almost embarrassed to admit that I've also done quite a bit of heli-skiing with clients who have those big fat wallets that are too heavy to keep carrying around. It's banned in France, of course. Their President Mitterrand decided to ban it, once he'd done enough himself and couldn't do any more. But it's great in Switzerland and Italy and New Zealand and places. Being a pure mountaineer, I don't really approve of going up in helicopters just so that wealthy people can ski back down off summits ... Well, not unless I'm joining in, of course ...

On one occasion I'd left a high mountain hut early with a group of clients and skinned and climbed up to a summit. At a flattish col just below the summit I knew the heli-skiers would be landing soon, so I told my team to leave their gear and rucksacks spread about on the snow, so that the chopper couldn't land. They had to drop off on a flat spot a few hundred metres lower instead, and we got the summit to ourselves. Okay! A bit of a dirty trick, but my guys had put in several hours of hard graft for that summit. I was just giving my friends a better value experience.

On one strange occasion a helicopter was really useful. We were skiing a steep variation of a big classic descent and traversed around a corner on to a big slope that I knew often had a double bergschrund at the bottom. But I hadn't been able to inspect it from below and we didn't know for sure if it was completely safe. A couple of posh-looking guys had followed us, and they clearly had local influence because while I pondered about going for it, they waved to a helicopter that was coming nearby. This guy obviously knew the pilot because he got his mobile phone out and while the chopper buzzed about and inspected everything, he gave us the okay. We went for it and there was a good snow bridge at the bottom that was skiable. I think my clients were quite impressed by the superior service they'd received.

As well as the traditional alpine climbing and ski-mountaineering, I've always done a fair bit of mixed winter climbing and technical ice climbs, right from the old easy stuff through to the modern steep frozen ice cascades. Sometimes there can be three types of ice all on one climb, if conditions are good. There can be old, hard frozen ice that takes good ice screws. Then there can be recent, creamy ice that takes terrific placements of modern ice axe picks; and then alongside that there can be odd ice sculptures, like cabbages, formed in the wind. You just drape big runner-slings over those as you climb past. But my favourite are icicle threads.

It's probably a sign of my age, from when we only had natural runners, but I still can't resist clipping a bit of ice and lashing a big sling around a good strong icicle.

Regarding teaching novices to lead ice climbs for themselves, I developed the system of leading a single pitch and leaving ice screws about every three metres with a one-and-a-half-metre-long sling attached. Novices could then top rope the pitch. Then I would encourage them to lead the pitch, clipping a runner every one and a half metres. Then they could lead the same pitch without the long slings and just clipping a runner every three metres. They soon progressed to six-metre runners and then to fixing their own. There are lots of winter venues around Europe where ice cascades are just like an outdoor climbing wall. During one day of instruction most clients can go from seconding their personal limit up to leading that same grade, whatever their personal standard.

After a five-day course of guiding I would often ask people on their last day if they wanted to lead a few pitches at their own new limit, or second something harder and beyond their previous experience. Surprisingly, many wanted to be extended, not to be gripped, but just to experience the next level of steepness and difficulty – often a big eye-opener for them.

If you're going on an extended trip with someone you need to know that they've got the right gear for the job – both hot and cold conditions. I've seen members of other groups with cold fingers and toes and also with hard white lumps of frostnip on tips of noses. Ski gloves are now so much better and more dextrous then old mitts, but being a thick northerner, I don't suffer from cold hands. So even for ice climbing I like to use grippy mountain bike gloves that are thin but waterproof, and so much better for threading those awkward icicles. In winter you've got to be able to do everything with gloves on. Not just pull up zips and clip karabiners, but work altimeters and even more delicate things. If you take gloves off, then put them inside a jacket. Don't let them fill with snow and definitely don't hold them between knees. A big puff of wind, legs come apart and gloves blow away; I've seen it loads of times.

Regarding footwear, I once got very cold toes in a 1960s winter storm while wearing thin workmen's boots. My big toes didn't blister but they went hard and white and I couldn't feel them for a whole six months. Eventually, I got 'hot aches', screaming pain for a whole week, as the nerve ends regenerated. The cure for hot aches is to stick the offending parts into snow or cold water to slow down the returning blood flow. Modern mountain boots are warm and dry and just brilliant.

On one Himalayan trip I used great big ski-touring boots with three pairs of socks and Gore-Tex thermal inners. The outer plastic shells only had two clips, so were easy to fasten, even with cold hands when half asleep at 1 a.m. With two Sherpas and three clients and a midnight start to a 6,000-metre plus summit day, I was the only one without cold toes until after the sun came up.

Goggles can also be a crucial bit of kit in snow, spindrift and bad weather, but they need to be looked after and used carefully. If goggles mist up, you can't see. If you can't see then you can't navigate. Than you get off-route and get lost. Then you get knackered and sit down. Then you get cold. And then you get dead. One tiny mistake in bad weather in the mountains often leads to an epic.

There is also a lot of mountain guiding to be done around other parts of the world. After I took some people up Mount Aspiring in New Zealand – the Matterhorn of the southern hemisphere – the whole group hired a six-seater aeroplane the next day to fly from Wanaka down to Milford Sound and the fjords. I told the pilot where we had been and he detoured over to Mount Aspiring and buzzed us in figure of eights around the summit so that they could see their own steps in the snow, right up on to the summit. Quite a treat for them.

Another time in New Zealand we were supposed to be climbing, but there had been a lot of rain in the valleys and the mountains were plastered with snow. I was with a guy who was a good skier, so we borrowed some boots and skis and helicoptered up to a hut near Mount Cook, at the base of Mount Elie de Beaumont, which is three peaks north of Mount Cook and has a big snowy south face. In New Zealand a lot of farmers have second-hand helicopters and use them to herd up their sheep and deer. They will drop you almost anywhere that you want to be, so you can ski anything. We went out to this farmer's helicopter and as we flew up we got into a bit of a snowstorm, so he set his machine on the mountainside on one runner with the rotor spinning until the wind eased off. Then we continued up higher so we could climb to the hut. This hut was just a garden shed really and would have blown away if it hadn't been tied down with wire cables.

We skinned up, then cramponed higher, and roped up for the top section. The first turns off the summit were a bit icy so we needed thirty metres of sideslipping on a rope, but then the ski descent down a big mountain face through sérac bands for a thousand metres was just brilliant. Then we stopped at the same hut to pick up our gear and have a brew.

We wound up a phone with a handle – which reminded me of my childhood at home – to order a plane from the bottom of the Tasman Glacier. There was some tricky skiing to get through a hundred metres more of ice cliffs and then about six miles of linking figure of eight turns in perfect spring snow down the Tasman Glacier. The Japanese tourist planes even flew low down to have a close look. Being November and early summer down south, we slowly sank deeper into the slush as we got lower. A bit of sloppy slush can be great fun to ski; it's just like skiing powder but a bit wetter. In fact, in Chamonix some of us revel in skiing 'slop'. But on this occasion it got wet and very deep, just before the boulder fields started. And then it started to rain. And then it turned to hailstones and suddenly got quite black. We thought there was no way a plane could come in for us and I had visions of shredded feet because I had bits of cardboard down the back of my heels to make the borrowed, downhill boots fit. It looked like a two-day walk out through the boulders.

Eventually, there was a little buzzing noise over Mount Cook and the Great Divide, and a little plane sank into the slush beside us. The pilot threw out two big shovels and screamed at us to dig like crazy. We floundered in front of the plane's skis, shovelling frantically while he revved the guts out of his motor, and we leapt in with the shovels, just as he managed to lift off, with hailstones rattling on the windscreen. Phew! What a relief. My companion was well chuffed at having skied the south face of one of the high peaks in New Zealand, because it had only been done four or five times before.

Once, we were high up somewhere, climbing an ice couloir at night. I've always been keen on crossing bergschrunds at about midnight. The ice is in better condition and there's less chance of stonefall. Also, it's a great experience for clients, doing routes safely and seeing dawn break as they get higher and higher. On this night there was a very bright full moon as we'd expected, and really thick cloud below us in the valley. It was almost like daylight. Now, we have probably all seen Brocken spectre in the mountains, when the sun has cast our shadows on to the clouds below and reflects a rainbow coloured halo around the shadow of our heads. I once saw a series of about six of them while scrambling along a ridge. But this experience was very different and quite stunning because it was 1 a.m. The bright full moon was casting our shadows on to the cloud below, leaving the most perfect lunar Brocken spectre, with the full coloured halo effect. We took photographs, so I haven't made this up, but lots of weather experts said afterwards that they didn't know that lunar ones were possible.

On one Himalayan expedition I had a group of seven people. Some were there to climb a peak and some to do the cultural trekking thing, and so we went up into the Langtang Valley in northern Nepal, through the Dhunche and Syafru villages, towards Langshisha Ri peak – that has a face with great big flutes of ice columns on it, all on the south side of Shishapangma. Later, while trekking up to our base camp, we stopped at the usual teahouses, and at one of them everybody bought a simple, colourful woven bracelet or belt. The lady, who was probably only about twenty-five, only wanted two and a half dollars for the whole lot, but of course, I gave her quite a bit more. But one guy didn't want to buy or wear anything. Funnily enough he was ill for nearly the whole trip and didn't get above 5,000 metres. Everyone else on that trip broke their personal altitude records and I got two of them up to our summit at just under 6,000 metres; all still wearing their Nepali bracelets, of course!

I've always told clients in my groups that we were all in a perfect democracy. Everyone could chat and discuss our plans and objectives. There was always a plan A and plan B and C, and everyone could put in their 'pennyworth'. However, in life-threatening epic situations it would always become an absolute dictatorship. On one occasion I had to say to someone, 'If you don't do what I say right now, we are both going to die tonight.' That's fairly decisive leadership and sometimes it's needed. Maybe it comes naturally from sixty-five years' experience of surviving in the mountains.

As a civil engineer and quarry operator, as well as a professional mountain guide, I was asked to go to the North Face of Everest in Tibet to do a 'feasibility study' and help design a high-altitude research hospital, especially as the ground might be unstable and the foundations were likely to be tricky. It was to be at north side Base Camp at 5,300 metres, above Rongbuk Monastery, and we were sort of guests of the Chinese Tibetan Mountaineering Association. We flew from Kathmandu to Lhasa by South China Airlines in a third-hand Swiss Boeing with about 300 seats. But there were only eleven of us on it, and they sat us all down one side by the windows. I thought the engines on the other side must be knackered and probably the wing as well. But the little Chinese pilot, who only looked about twelve years old, even though his uniform was dripping in gold braid and medals, must have known where we were going because he buzzed us in circles around the summit of Everest and over the North Ridge. It was all very impressive out of our side windows.

The idea at Everest Base Camp was to check out a suitable, stable location and to design this little research hospital of just a few rooms. I think the Chinese authorities wanted a hotel and cafe to make money, but climbers want a hospital for treating high-altitude casualties. Regarding the location, the glaciers are receding even in the Himalaya. Glaciers were stable in New Zealand for a few years, but they are receding as well now. The Base Camp location used to be a lake from glacial meltwater, but it must have filled in with glacial rock debris and then filled in with river-washed gravel. The prevailing winds must have washed sands and gravels up on to the lee shore a long time ago, and so now there is a fairly level area like a beach or shelf of gritty sand. Higher up the valley there is still movement in the icy moraine heaps, but this beach area is flat and looks to be fairly stable. Because there is no real vegetation there is no rotting organic matter and so there is no topsoil, but in this beach area there are tiny plants and their root systems are struggling for nutrients. So the roots are two- and three-feet deep. The bits of plants have been struggling for years, so the ground is not moving. It is stable and would support a building.

We met a guy who was supposed to be the chief engineer at the Chinese Ministry of Geology in Tibet, but he didn't know the first thing about rocks or glaciation, so we assumed that he was spying on our work to see what we did. We did some tests and trials and dug some test pits – or at least a couple of our Sherpas did, because pick and shovel work at 5,300 metres is not a picnic – and I showed that a floating concrete foundation slab would be stable and support the weight of a building just as in earthquake areas. All we would need would be a few four-wheel-drive lorries and loads of cement. There are millions of tonnes of concreting sand and aggregates available there, and we could make concrete blocks and dressed stone blocks using Nepali stonemasons. The building would be two storeys high with about ten hospital rooms, with tapered and curved walls like a Tibetan monastery, and we even checked the potential orientation with the boss monk down at the monastery, because the entrance door had to face a certain direction.

There were several expeditions there in that year, but I wasn't registered as a climber with the liaison officers, and so wasn't on any permit. But, being a climber, I couldn't resist a bit of a walkabout. I borrowed some gear and sneaked off up to Intermediate Camp and then up to Advanced Base Camp. Then, even though I wasn't acclimatised for more than about 6,000 metres, I went straight on up to the North Col. Alison Hargreaves was there at the same time, and being fully acclimatised she stormed past me while I was struggling with borrowed gear. I knew that I would suffer if I pushed on or stayed high for too long while unacclimatised, so I staggered straight back down all the way to Base Camp that same day. That's about twenty-five kilometres horizontally past two other camps, as well as the vertical up and down.

It was another 4 a.m. to 11 p.m. day, and again I was pretty wacked out. Nineteen hours continuous on just one Mars Bar again. The next night we had a guy from another group who was on a commercial climbing expedition and we could hear him wheezing and gurgling in his tent. He was suffering from the usual breathing problems and drowning in fluid in his lungs. We had a Gamow Bag with us, which is a portable altitude chamber, but with a Perspex window. We got him inside and used the foot pump to pressurise him up from the equivalent of 5,300 metres down to sea level. Each time he recovered he panicked to be let out, so we had to deflate, unzip and let him out. Then he would deteriorate and gurgle again. Two of us spent all night repeatedly pumping him up to sea-level pressure and then releasing him. The next morning he was still in a bad way and we had to put him on oxygen and then evacuate him down to lower altitude.

When we got back to Europe, we built a model of our proposed hospital and my feasibility study was translated into French and then into Chinese. Unfortunately, it was all confiscated by the Chinese and I believe they've built a rough concrete shed lower down the valley now, but I don't think it's doing any hospital work.

Before I left Everest, a guiding colleague of mine was training a client who had very little experience to go there and try to climb it. (I wish the media wouldn't use the word 'conquer'.) In the initial days, this client tried to fit his crampons upside down on his boots. That is with the points facing up, thinking they might be dangerous with the points downwards. This sounds a bit unlikely, but it was true, and shows just how precarious it is taking inexperienced people into high and dangerous mountains.

In extremis, good decisions have to be made quickly and instinctively. The whole idea of high mountain expeditions being commercialised is open to debate. The best operations work on the basis of one client to one professional at high altitude, and even then not many folk can look after themselves up there. Very few can look after someone else as well.

While on the theme of high-altitude stuff, I once took a group of research doctors and medical students up to a high alpine hut and looked after them while they took samples from climbers passing through and did genetic testing. Their research eventually showed that about ten per cent of the population has a gene that allows them to acclimatise okay. But about ten per cent of the population has a gene that stops them acclimatising at all.

At one time I used to give a lecture on diet and nutrition for endurance mountaineering. Nothing too technical, just the basics, and it was based on three parts.

The first was from sophisticated gym work in America with subjects wired up for everything in and everything out. They measured that we use one or two calories per minute just sleeping, about four calories per minute walking about, maybe about six per minute running or cycling, and up to eight to ten calories per minute if you are scrambling uphill using arms as well as legs and certainly if carrying a big rucksack, maybe rushing a bit and maybe when it's cold and at low atmospheric pressure.

Then for the second part, I related this to a twenty-four-hour day in the mountains. On an expedition you might be carrying big loads up to altitude for maybe six to eight hours a day. Amateur alpinists might leave a hut at 3 a.m. and walk up a glacier with a rucksack, and then climb from 6 a.m. to 3 p.m., sometimes at about nine calories a minute with a bit of belaying at only four per minute. Then they night abseil and descend and walk down until maybe 10 p.m. at a rate of say six calories per minute. If you are guiding professionally you might be working hard for only six hours a day but that might be every day for several weeks or even month. Simple arithmetic shows that 'endurance mountaineering' can burn 5,000 to 8,000 calories per day, and maybe on occasions 10,000 calories or more.

The third part of this study is from diet books. Tomatoes have about two calories per ounce – probably less energy than it takes to eat it. Boiled potatoes or bread have about fifty calories per ounce. I guess chips or bacon butties have about 100 calories. Even if we eat forty ounces of chocolate per day, which is probably impossible, then we still can't take in enough calories for hard continuous mountaineering days. Some of us have had twenty-four hours in one push on occasions, and you simply can't eat enough. Certainly, after big climbing trips we always lost weight and then stopped at motorway services three times a day, for three-course meals and double chips with everything.

One guiding colleague swears by lots of cola and salty crisps on the hill. I quite like butter and cheese on top of chocolate biscuits, and maybe a bit of jam on top as well. Personally, at high altitude I have survived on aspirins and Liquorice Allsorts with a handful of snow and, critically, as many brews as you can get.

In concluding the theme of this chapter, for me, my favourite guiding is skiing off summits with a couple of competent clients. Sit in the sun on the top and wait for your chosen line to soften into good spring snow and then go for it. Some of the best ski days are doing the big off-piste runs, directly accessible from the lifts in the Chamonix Valley, with nice folk who are regular clients. The prestigious Pas De Chevre, under the north face of the Dru down into Chamonix, or the Grande Envers Du Plan and its variations off the top of the Midi.

Probably my best week of ski-mountaineering guiding, several years ago, was skiing from just under the summit rocks of the Gran Paradiso in Italy. Then, the next day, off the summit of the Aiguille d'Argentière and then two days later off the top of Mont Dolent – the border of three countries, in fabulous spring snow, all the way back down to the cars. This was followed by another two-day trip and a descent off the top of Mont Blanc. Not bad for seven days with clients and not bad at the age of sixty-five!

I always advise young guides that mountain guiding is just like any other business and the same rules apply. Don't waste ten per cent of your time and money on advertising; just give folks a ten per cent better value experience and you'll have regular clients for life.

Peter and Sylvie with Peter Williams at Rhoscolyn, May 1998. © Peter Allison Collection

Chapter 10
OLD FRIENDS

Eleven years after my younger brother's first artificial aorta graft, he suffered another heart attack. A young hotshot surgeon had cut away all the old congealed tissues and tried to repeat the operation with a new graft. We had been brothers and good mates. We'd built cars together and we'd rallied cars together. We'd climbed a bit and worked together for years.

When ill, his ambition had been to ski the Vallée Blanche together, even though he wasn't very good, and we did so, but with quite a struggle. Near the bottom he went very pale and sat down and said his pulse had dropped to thirty, because he could hear the metal valve that they'd put in his heart during the first heart and aorta operation. I thought he'd had it and he started to go blue, but then after about fifteen minutes he suddenly picked up. His ticker had started up again and we very slowly got him down. Much later, after the second artificial aorta transplant, he came round from the operation for a bit, but then he simply didn't survive the second open-chest surgery. Eventually, the machines were switched off.

As is clear from what I have written so far, I had a very good relationship with my younger brother, who was a friend as well as a sibling. Indeed, I have been blessed in having a number of really close friends. Three in particular: Peter Williams, who I met at university, and more recently my fellow guides Dave Alcock and David Hopkins, each of whom have shared many of the adventures described in these pages. Then there are those friends who I have met through climbing and with whom I have also shared good times and challenging exploits.

In the 1950s I met Paul Nunn when he was still a wee lad. We were both dossing in a barn in Borrowdale and we went off and did a new route together on one of the Borrowdale crags. We never wrote it up anywhere because we weren't really bothered, but many years later someone else had claimed it as a first ascent in a new guidebook. We were quite surprised that they didn't realise somebody had climbed up there previously, because Paul's granny had just bought him some proper climbing gear and we'd left a big fat, obvious piton in the second pitch. Paul had also been a biker. He said that he'd always kept equality between his motorbike falls and his rock climbing falls, but when he got to fifteen of each he thought that he'd better sell the motorbike. Sadly, Paul didn't return from one of his many mountaineering expeditions.

John Clements was one of the hotshot rock climbers of the 1960s and we had some great climbing days together – he'd done his chemistry degree at Durham University and then we were neighbours in Liverpool together while he did his PhD research. He was very posh and very loud, and his parties were way over the top. The punches and cocktails came straight out of his chemistry laboratory and were lethal. However, I must say that I never came across any kind of drug use while I was an undergraduate or throughout the 1960s – I reckon that climbing was a substitute for almost everything else in life, and we used to consider that climbing wasn't a recreation or hobby; it was a full-on way of life. John was fantastic on rock, but unfortunately he didn't survive an introductory Scottish winter weekend in the snow and ice.

Many years later, I was in a pub with Chris Dale and another good climbing friend. I just happened to mention that when I was fifteen years old I'd cycled up to Fort William and gone in the Ben Nevis race. He said that when he was fifteen years old he bunked off school one Thursday and hitched up to the Isle of Hoy and soloed the Old Man of Hoy pinnacle and then hitched back home. However, the ferry was delayed so he missed school on the Monday as well. His father was a policeman in Penrith so he got a rollicking from his father as well as from his headmaster. Anyway, the other pal then said that when he was fifteen he had hitched out to Zermatt and soloed the Matterhorn. Blimey, at fifteen years old! After that I never bragged about doing anything, ever again. Whatever you've achieved there's always someone who's done more, bigger and better, and faster, or younger, or older, or on one leg or something.

I'd done a few routes with Chris in Wales and we'd also done a couple of climbs together in the Alps. We'd also done *Gemini* together on Ben Nevis when it was a bit thin. My pitch was just a steep, thin column of brittle ice, but his pitch was so desperate and precarious he must have led it by levitation. There was lots of twisting and torquing of ice-axe picks in very thin cracks and lots of very marginal moves.

Once, in the 'good old days,' I hitch-hiked from Sheffield to Llanberis with a coil of electrical wire and a pair of pliers and rewired an old banger that had burnt out the previous weekend. I met up with a climbing mate, Tom Hurley, who was a rough and ready biker from Lancashire. In the afternoon, we drove up the pass and decided to do *The Cromlech Girdle* – in the boots than we just happened to be wearing. When we got around to *Left Wall*, I fixed a runner high up in the crack and then belayed across in *Cenotaph Corner*. Tom, as causal as usual, fell off the first move and hurtled all the way across in a pendulum, just about kicking me in the teeth with his big boots. Afterwards, I sold my rewired old banger to one of his mates for a few quid, but then I had to hitch a lift back home to Sheffield. That was quite a big day.

I climbed with Laurie Holliwell several times. Laurie was another absolutely top rock climber of the late 1960s, so I think he only climbed with me for the drives. But when we did *Dinosaur* together on Gogarth (named because you needed a small brain and a long neck), it was his turn to drive. The climb back then was really scary on the steep, loose, brittle quartzite rock, but the drive back in his Cortina GT was absolutely terrifying. He could overtake on all three sides: nearside, offside, and over the top if necessary. He overtook three cars at once by going around the wrong side of a roundabout, cutting them up and forcing one off the road. When he eventually 'totalled' that car it was on the never-ending left-hander near Llangollen and he ricocheted off the stone walls for half a mile before accepting that it was a terminal write-off.

We did the second ascent of *The Skull* together, but we got rained off after two pitches, so we went back the next day to do the top pitch. I think Laurie felt he needed my long legs to bridge up the top, wide overhanging groove. We went to the top of the crag and he just put a line sling around a couple of rocks on the scree that just happened to be touching, and threw the abseil ropes over into space. I said, 'What on earth are you doing, Laurie? If you abseil off that you won't ever need a pension.' I put about six anchor slings on everything I could find and equalised them, and then we abseiled over.

It was still the days of using a figure-of-eight sit sling (we hadn't yet invented harnesses) and hawser-laid ropes over the shoulder for friction. It was all a bit precarious and painful on big free abseils when well clear and away from overhanging rock. The ropes slowly stretched and twisted around and dug into the shoulder. Eyes were closed, body spinning around slowly, light then dark through your closed eyelids. We completed the climb okay, but Laurie never did learn to abseil safely and tragically died as a result of an abseiling accident, so he never did get that pension.

One cracking Scottish winter weekend, I did one of the great classics on Creag Meagaidh with Nick Estcourt, in typical Scottish conditions. We got to the top of the climb at night in total whiteout, blackout conditions and traversed around the top to where we both thought *Easy Gully* should be – or might be – and hacked through a big cornice. Then we sat on our rucksacks, crossed our fingers, hoping that this really was where *Easy Gully* might be, and sledged down into black oblivion.

A few years later Nick and I were in the Climbers' Club hut after a good day on Cloggy. Nick was a powerful mountaineer and he still had superfluous energy and half an hour left to do something more. I suggested *Hangover*, which I'd done several times before, but there was a general guffaw from the residents and before we knew it we were landed in a £10 bet to be back in the hut within thirty minutes. We sprinted up the diagonal path to the crag with one rope and two slings, and Nick shot up the first pitch. When he'd gone about six metres I gathered up lots of coils of rope and followed up behind him. By the time he was belayed I was alongside him. I dropped the coils and shot up the wall along the traverse line, up the top crux groove, around a tree and dragged the rope along to the abseil tree that was there in those days. In moments Nick was up and across and we'd abseiled down. I dragged the abseil rope down and ran down the scree, coiling it roughly as we ran. As we collapsed into the hut the adjudicator consulted the timekeeper's watch and grumpily declared twenty-eight minutes. However, as they were all tight-fisted climbers, we never did get our £10 winnings from them. Sadly, he is another good friend who never returned. He died in an avalanche on K2 in 1978.

I remember where I first met Ben Wintringham in Snowdonia one winter, when he was about sixteen. We glissaded down a snow-filled gully off Y Garn with some other folk. He was already a brilliant rock climber but I'm not sure he'd been in the snow before, so it wasn't really fair on him, glissading down manky, slushy gullies. Later on, I think he was a bit jealous of my Lotus and after he inherited lots of dosh from his American mother, he bought an E-Type then a Ferrari and then a series of seven Porsches. One Friday night I came over the Welsh moors from Merseyside on to the A5 just as Ben was coming up from London in one of his Porsches. We had a cracking blast in convoy along the straights at a leisurely 130 and then scrubbed off a bit of rubber on the Betws-y-Coed bends.

After Smiler and I did the Eiger together, we were invited on a sponsored trip to South Africa by one of their TV channels, to compare themselves to European climbers, I suppose. I had fancied climbing in their Drakensberg mountains, but even though the trip was a freebie I didn't want to be used for their political situation, so we cancelled the whole thing. Instead, at the last minute, we were sponsored by British Leyland and a vodka company to do some routes on the Rock of Gibraltar, and Ben came with us. The navy had recently taken the old naval guns out of the tunnels in the Rock and had decommissioned everything, so some Spanish climbers had gone there to do first ascents. They'd fallen off, of course, and a Spaniard had been helicoptered off by the RAF with a broken thigh. I think it was a prestige thing, because the navy were doing the first sea trials of their new Harrier Jump Jets on their new 'invincible' aircraft carrier, so they clearly wanted Brits to do the first climbs on the cliffs.

Ben and I had an RAF jet pilot in our team, and Smiler had Don Whillans had a navy man in their team. Smiler and his team did a route but got benighted because the rock is steep and loose and 460 metres high – and also quite difficult. They spent a very cold night on a little ledge in just T-shirts and shorts. When I started up our route, I was laying away against a thin, friable edge. We had expected decent limestone, but it was crumbly chalk and pieces were snapping off – I was dropping handholds over my shoulder on to the TV crews. We would have come down if it hadn't been for the TV cameras and the fact that someone was paying for everything.

Ben led some desperate pitches, and the military guys imposed upon us were completely spaced out with eyes out on stalks – except for the times when their eyes were tight shut. I led up an overhanging groove pushing loose blocks back into the crag, and bridged out about eight feet wide.

Then I got up to an old gun window with rusty bars across a grille. The TV commentators said that we had also been stuck, benighted and spent a shivering night out on an exposed ledge. The truth is that I had climbed through the bars, and our navy pilot came into his own. We went down the narrow tunnels to the officer's mess – where only he could buy the drinks – and then a nightclub, and we spent the night visiting all sorts of bars. The next morning, he took us back up to the same little window and we climbed out and had a shake out for the cameras. Ben was always the last man to leave a good party. But again, very sadly, he is another good climbing friend who didn't survive an abseiling incident.

Once when it was lashing down with Welsh rain and we climbers were bored and playing darts in the pub, seven of us decided to go and get wet and do something easy that we could definitely manage, even in these conditions. We would just walk up Snowdon, the easy way. We were seven experienced alpinists and mountaineers, and the other six all had big reputations. There was Pete Boardman, who I'd climbed with on gritstone because he was at Nottingham University a few years after me, together with his Himalayan climbing mate Joe Tasker. Then there was Nick Estcourt and Mick Burke as well, and others who were all good friends. But the problem was the weather: because it was deep winter there had been lots of heavy snow and it was blowing an absolute blizzard on the hill. We couldn't actually see anything. We got lost. We couldn't find any path. We all kept falling through the snowdrifts into deep holes between big boulders. But the point is that they were all really nice guys and all good mates, and the other six were all outstanding mountaineers. Yet the mountain didn't know that they were all famous mountaineers and unfortunately, it saddens us all, but the six friends from that day all failed to return from their final big Himalayan expeditions, and they are all no longer with us.

However, it hasn't only been British climbing friends who have departed. Back in the early 1980s, before I bust my pelvis, we had interviewed Patrick Vallençant, the French pioneering extreme skier, for a ski video, in Argentière. He had a lot of black hair and a lot of black beard, and icy blue eyes. He was wild, and looked like a wolf. I climbed with him a bit because he wanted to do a rock route on the Midi. I mentioned to him that I'd done the first British ascent of the *Couturier Couloir* back in 1967, and he said 'Puh! So?' He wasn't very impressed of course, because he'd done the first ski descent of it, and it is about fifty-five degrees in places.

After that, I had a stunning day skiing with him down a line that we can't do now because of the glaciers retreating, and it's always bare blue ice and fifty-degree granite rock slab. Needless to say, granite is a bit tricky to get a ski edge on. Every time I look at this descent now I wonder how on earth I got down it. I guess I was on my limit then, and afterwards he said, 'I think you need better ski shoes!' I was using some weird Swiss boots with a turn-buckle at the front that pulled a wire that, in turn, pulled the heel down into the heel of the boot. They fitted the foot quite well in one part of the foot, but not at all in about ten other parts of the foot. Actually, what he probably meant to say, translated into his loose English, was 'You're a crap skier – better stick to the pistes!' He was rock climbing in southern France when he fell. The rope reversed across a banana-shaped karabiner and came out, and he hit the deck.

Ken was an elderly ski client who wanted to do the Vallée Blanche with his younger wife. He had been quite ill, so I had carried his skis and some walking bits and looked after him especially carefully. He had a fantastic chalet with a double garage in the valley. One day he had been cutting hedges and had lit a bonfire and then gone inside for a power nap. The neighbours' kids then banged on his door, but he didn't understand their rapid French and basically told them to bugger off because he was tired. When the fine engine came around the corner he suddenly realised that his second garage was on fire. Nowadays, when someone is trying to help a friend in need and their help is being declined we refer to it as a 'you can bugger off moment'. He also passed away in the mountains, but not because of an avalanche or accident. He had a massive heart attack in his eighties, in the middle of a big red run, and unfortunately the helicopter medical team couldn't resuscitate him.

I cannot leave this chapter without another reference to my older brother. When he stopped climbing in the late 1960s, he worked obsessively and fairly ruthlessly in business, and when he retired at sixty-nine, he started sailing. His first ever trip in a sailboat was right around Britain and his second trip, in his seventies, was across the Atlantic. After that we managed to sit in the same room together for long enough to arrange our ninety-eight-year-old mother's funeral.

Then he must have studied the Arctic ice images, because he was the first person to sail a fibreglass boat through the Northwest Passage, around Greenland, North Canada and Alaska. Coming back down the North Pacific he was hit by a storm and while he was up the mast trying to fix it, the Alaskan fisherman that he had hired to be his crewman took his satellite phone and rang a Mayday. They were rescued by an Alaskan trawler, and when my brother's wrecked boat was washed up on the coast he bought another one with the insurance money. I think his hero was Tilman, who was a mountaineer turned sailor who sailed off into the sunset on his own, in the southern oceans. So later on, my brother did the Northwest Passage again at about seventy-five years old, and just kept on going around the North Russian coast. But the Russians wouldn't let him land because he'd been in trouble with a Russian court the year before, so he stayed on board from Greenland all the way around the Arctic Ocean until back in Norway. That took him about twelve weeks and knowing him he probably lived on tins of tomato soup. It must have been cold, wet, foggy and scary with icebergs everywhere.

The trip hit the headlines in all the international sailing magazines and made him quite famous, which is maybe what he wanted, but of course it killed him. On his return to Britain he was taken straight into intensive care with kidney and liver failure. Then he got Hodgkin lymphoma and they operated; then he got pleurisy and finally pneumonia. The doctors said that any one of these would have killed a normal person. At his funeral, a north-eastern farmer that I used to know saw all the people and said he hadn't realised my brother had so many friends. I told him that he hadn't really. It was just that nobody would do anything with him twice, so he had to keep finding new folk. That may sound a bit derogatory, but I think he would have been quite chuffed and proud that everyone was talking about him. A climbing friend's wife said that he'd been quite nice to her once, in a mountain hut, when she'd had a headache. His chest puffed out and he said, 'Oh! I've never been accused of being "nice" before.'

But now, in the summer of 2016, I've got to add another one to this chapter. Another friend and old neighbour, Ralph, a six-foot-seven-inch German guide, was climbing Mont Blanc with two Polish clients when an ice sérac cliff collapsed on Mont Maudit just at the wrong moment when they were underneath it. He was a lovely man, always a big smile, a fantastic rock climber and fabulous skier and snowboarder.

It's so upsetting, losing so many good friends.

Chevalier Couloir. © Peter Allison Collection

Chapter 11
OLD AGE

When I was young I used to say, 'There's a couple of blokes 300 metres above us; we'll catch them up in half an hour and get past them, so that they can't knock rocks on to us.' Now I say, 'There's a couple of blokes 300 metres below us; let's sit down for a rest and let them climb past.' It's called old age.

In your twenties you can get super-fit in a couple of days of hard work, but in your forties, it takes about six months of proper training. When you're over seventy it just doesn't happen. Now by the time I get the muscles worked up, I'm knackered. So now in my mid-seventies I have stopped guiding professionally and stopped paying my professional insurance. Why would anyone want to go out on the hill with an 'oldie'? I just carry on doing the same stuff – climbing and skiing – with mates and ex-clients who have become good friends.

I now climb with mates who are also in their seventies and even eighties. If we climb through younger teams who ask if we've done this route before, we hesitate then say, 'Yeah! Fifty-odd years ago.' Sometimes I say 'No,' and then suddenly recognise a particular shaped handhold that I know I must have used before. We are all now in the 'Can't Remember Club'. One eighty-five-year-old pal went to the doctor and told him he was out of breath. When the doctor asked him when was it that he was out of breath the pal replied it was when he was chasing his grandson uphill on his mountain bike.

I still quite like mixed winter climbs in thin conditions. A hardish route in excellent conditions is obviously just brilliant; but an easy route in really desperate thin conditions can be a real buzz as well. I think that I've been very lucky and fortunately, when I was pushing seventy, I was still able to lead *The Peapod* at Curbar and *Sirplum* in Cheedale which are on totally different types of rock, gritstone and limestone, and both still Derbyshire 5bs.

Many years ago, I had quite fancied trying to be the oldest pensioner to lead *Right Wall* on Dinas Cromlech. Young climbing rockstars had told me that there were big 'jug' handholds on it, but to me, that meant tiny, two-fingertips crimps. I had done a bit of the modern training lark, but every time I managed to get mean and lean, I seemed to catch a cold.

When I was a youth, we thought that training was a bit overrated. We used to go to the pub and then go climbing. And then we'd go back to the pub. When the next generation of climbers started to train for it in the gym and then later on at climbing walls, we thought it was almost like cheating. After all, the whole thing then was supposed to be just a part-time hobby. Actually, the training doesn't make me stronger anyway. It makes me tired. It's the recovery that makes me stronger. Back then, one of the older guys said that if you climbed a lot, then 'the best form of training was to rest.'

About ten years ago in my mid-sixties I suffered a serious eye problem. We had been cragging on the sea cliffs of Devon, and driving back up the motorway I realised that my vision was strange. Normally you can see out sideways at nearly ninety degrees, but I was only seeing at about forty-five degrees out to the front of my right eye. So I pulled over and slowed right down and next morning located a specialist in a private surgery. As I explained my symptoms to a receptionist, a voice shouted through the open door of another room, 'Tell him to sit down and keep very, very still.' The white coat came in, examined my eye, and said the symptoms were exactly those of a detached retina in the eye. I said, 'Thank you very much,' and got up to walk out and this guy shouted, 'No! No, No. Sit down. Stay very still – you must not move. I'll get you into Liverpool eye hospital. Now. Immediately. This afternoon.'

He asked if I'd had a really bad bump or a car crash. Well, I've had about forty or fifty cars and spun nearly all of them at some stage or other and maybe even 'scratched' a couple, but not for quite a long time. When I was young I worked with a lunatic guy who liked to show off, especially when leaving saloons of liquid refreshment. I was once a passenger with him when we left the road for a while and hit a kerb head-on. His Mini Cooper S cleared a little wall and pruned the tops off some old lady's rose bed. The headlight marks were about a metre up a solid stone wall at the back of her gardens.

Mind you, that's not necessarily the scariest lift I've ever been given. Once we were on a bus somewhere in the mountains of the world. This bus was a normal length, but the wheelbase was very short. That means the wheel axles were close together in the middle so that it could turn very tight around hairpin bends. Trouble is, this meant front and back were overhanging the side of the road. We were descending a steep mountain road with tight hairpins and sitting right in the back seats. As we descended at perilous speed, the driver's mobile phone went off. He slowed to a stop right on a bend and had a huge row with his wife on the phone. We were left quivering in the back of this shocking bus with the wheels only just on the edge of the road. He was shouting and screaming, and we were balanced precariously way out the back, overhanging a huge gaping void.

The detached retina operation is extremely tricky and delicate. They have to put very thick oil inside the eyeball with a needle, which acts like a splint and keeps it all in place temporarily. How do I know this? Well, because they keep you awake and chat to you! It's actually a teaching hospital and was full of trainee surgeons and nurses, and the whole thing was quite amusing with lots of banter and Scouse-type humour. They had to try and stop me from chuckling!

It took about six weeks for this thick oil to disperse through the blood circulation and for the natural eye fluid to return. In the meantime, I lay permanently on one side, to stop the retina rolling back off. I was allowed to move for only five minutes in every hour, for two weeks, just for the necessities of life. I asked if I could accumulate the five-minute spells and go climbing for an hour. That was a very definite NO, so I watched Wimbledon sideways for two weeks. The funny thing is that with thick oil inside the eye you see everything very strangely. The images are all distorted – bigger and smaller, and upside down. As the thick oil disperses, part of the image you see is too big and upside down, and part is normal; and there's a strange strip of nothing across the middle.

After a few weeks I went back for a check-up, with my good eye covered. A bloke in a white coat walked into the room, or at least a vague blur walked into the room, and apparently held up a huge board with an enormous letter A on it and said, 'Can you read this?' I shuffled forward, reaching my hands out in front to feel and said, 'What? Where? Who are you? Who am I? Where am I? What am I doing here?' etc, etc. It's funny now, but it was very serious at the time. It was a very clever bit of surgery and thankfully it was a great success and my vision is now tickety-boo again.

But other stuff is just as important as the climbing now. My wife and constant companion Sylvie and I go around the world in our campervan and scramble up a few peaks and ski a few slopes and see a lot of wildlife in 'them there' hills. The kea birds, for example, in New Zealand are very amusing. They are big brightly coloured parrots that have a taste for some kind of chemical that is in rubber. We woke up once to find them eating the windscreen wipers on our rented campervan, although they prefer the softer rubber around the window frames. Apparently, they used to peck at the rubber petrol pipes underneath old VW vans. They seem to be very bright mentally as well. The rumour goes that one kea bird sat on the rail around a climbing hut watching climbers slide the door bolt back and forward to lock and unlock the door. After a bit of study, the thing flew across and slid the bolt in with its powerful beak while two climbers were inside, and locked them in for two days. I even saw two New Zealand climbers drying their alpine gloves on the balcony of a mountain hut and a kea bird watched them and then flew across, picked up the gloves, flew across the glacier and dropped them down a crevasse. I actually loaned them some spare thin ones. The big daft parrot flew back and perched there with a big grin on its face.

As for four-legged creatures, we've seen a few, especially in North America. One day we drove over a mountain pass and there in a layby was a great big brown grizzly, munching on berries. I screeched to a stop and ran back with the camera, merrily clicking away. Then suddenly, when I was about six metres away from the bear, a park ranger in his oversized truck drove in between the bear and me with an even more oversized gun sticking out of the passenger window. He shouted, 'If that bear wants you he'll have you,' and I very rapidly came to my senses. Bears can run faster than us, swim faster than us, climb trees faster than us and according to that ranger they can do calculus mathematics faster than us as well.

Even more impressive than the bear incident was seeing a mountain lion in Yosemite, and the park rangers said it was impossible because they are very rare and cautious and only come out at night. But we've got the photos. We were coming down from Half Dome and Yosemite Falls late in the day and instead of taking the main path we followed a very vague track next to the river, at dusk. Maybe it was because we needed a drink, but just as likely because we were knackered and lost. As I came around a corner among dense trees, there in the gloom about five metres away was a mountain lion with big, triangular, pointy ears. It stared at me for a bit – fairly bored, to be honest – and I stared back at it for a bit – fairly scared, to be honest – and then I took three photos in the dusk. Then it just casually turned away and slunk down to the river for a drink.

And now that's enough about wild creatures, so back to North America, where it has to be said that they've got it all: the climbing, the skiing, the winter ice climbing, the scenery, the temperatures, the lot. Once, we were in Death Valley at over 40 °C, on a day when a German tourist died of dehydration while trying to walk through the sandstone dunes and got lost. Two days later we were on Mount Whitney in the snow, and the next day we got stuck in a snow blizzard trying to cross a mountain pass.

My USA ambition used to be to get stopped for speeding by a US cowboy sheriff with his gun out, and eventually we were. But it wasn't for going too fast, it was for going too slow, in a great big lumbering American campervan. This thing had a six-metre overhang behind the back axle and a permanent log-burning 'furnace' in it. It had a big V8 engine that only did ten miles to the gallon and just had a poxy three-speed automatic gearbox. It was always in the wrong gear – uphill and downhill – and would only do fifty miles per hour flat out. You cannot rent small campervans in the States and these big ones are very comfortable and brilliant to live in, but they are absolute pigs to drive.

On this occasion we were cruising across Nevada on a straight, narrow road with dozens of trucks behind that wouldn't overtake. Suddenly there was a fat state trooper behind us on an even fatter Harley-Davidson with his blue flashing light on. He waved us on to the grass and then approached with his hand very obviously on his gun. He said we should have pulled over, but there was no hard shoulder and I argued that in Britain we weren't allowed to stop on motorway hard shoulders anyway, unless it was an emergency etc. After a long rollicking he threatened to lock us up, but then bizarrely as we left he gave us his business card and said to ring him if we had any more trouble in his state. Maybe it was secret code for asking for a tip.

As it happens we did have a bit more of an incident in Nevada. Late one night we were looking for somewhere to park up, so we pulled off at an interchange and drove along a dark narrow lane. There were a couple of old American trailers parked that looked decidedly dodgy, so we carried on and eventually parked in a layby in the pitch dark. The next morning, we woke up surrounded by five-metre-high barbed-wire fences, decorated around the top with some very stylish coils of razor wire. We were parked in the entrance of a state penitentiary prison under a big sign that said 'Keep Away

– Federal Correctional Institution.'

Once, in the States with a monster rented campervan, I 'bumped' into a car wash before returning the vehicle to the hire company and the deposit was equally monstrous. So I did a bit of an improvised respray job. The trouble was that it was covered in huge plastic transfers of rodeo cowboys and hot air balloons, all painted in red, white and blue. I unscrewed some angle iron trim off the back corner where it had got bent and bashed it straight with a rock, using a manhole cover as an anvil. Then I filled in the dents with flour and water paste. So then Picasso here, used white tooth-paste, borrowed red lipstick and blue mascara and carefully repainted and covered up the damage. I wouldn't recommend buying any of my second-hand cars, by the way.

Doing the North Face of the Eiger all those years ago was quite life-changing. Maybe more so than climbing a normal technical alpine route. First of all it's a big face, about 1,500 metres vertical with lots of traversing, so maybe 2,000 metres of climbing, and more like a Himalayan climb or like soloing a big route. When you're at Death Bivouac halfway up, it's a long way up to the top, but it's also an awful long way to get back down and there's a huge amount of history there. It's like being in the middle of the Atlantic Ocean in a rowing boat. Commitment like that changes you in your approach to work and to relationships – and to your whole attitude to a way of life.

After doing the Eiger, I remember people asking why we do such things, and I remember saying quite simply, 'Because we can.' I don't think it's that complicated, really. All right, it's a great personal 'buzz' to accomplish some-thing that maybe someone else can't do, and it's certainly satisfying to be the best you can be and reach your own full potential, but I still think it's all very simple: we do it because we can.

It helps to be blessed with good genes. The modern sports superstars are very specific shapes for their chosen activities. I know rock climbers whose arms are the same diameter as their legs and I know fell runners who have legs right up to their armpits. In my case, though, my father's family all died young, of heart attacks and strokes, and too much good living on wartime fags and bottles of whisky. My mother, when I asked her at ninety-seven if she wanted to be buried or cremated, said very dramatically, 'I don't want either, dear.' Her family all battled on until they were ninety-eight or ninety-nine, and had all lived quite simply. Maybe it was because of not enough 'good living'. As I say, it's all in the genes.

For a while now, I've said that I'd like a third of my ashes thrown over the top of The Pinnacle on Cloggy; a third scattered over the top of *The Sloth* at the Roaches; and then another third spread, with the wind, in a winter storm off the viewing platform at the very top of Grands Montets in Argentière. All three places are like my own personal back garden. Another third may as well just go in the wheelie bin. However, there seems to be a bit of a problem with this idea, and it isn't just the arithmetic, because having been in a proper fire, for real, in my forties I definitely don't fancy being incinerated, at least not too soon. So, I guess it's a dilemma for nearest and dearest. I suppose a disposable cardboard box under a tree, somewhere with a view of the hills, would be best.

Some recent research in the business world has shown that many successful business people had terrible relationships with their fathers, or that their fathers had died when they themselves were still young. Many business people are driven and trying to prove themselves to somebody, and so are many well-known climbers, mountaineers and steep skiers.

Personally, I have always felt that if I had had the choice of being the very best mountaineer, or still being able to be dragged up easy routes when I'm ninety, I would always have chosen to be able to potter up things when old, whereas many very top climbers stop dramatically when they think they can no longer be the very best.

Actually, I think it's quite a privilege to be allowed to grow old – even if it is disgracefully. I now have a T-shirt that says, 'The older I get, the better I used to be'. Recently, a couple of us skied a variation line off the top of the Aiguille d'Argentière in nice spring snow conditions, which is a good forty-five degrees plus, and probably pushing fifty degrees steep. My brother and I climbed this same line one summer, in slightly icy conditions, by chopping steps all the way up it, using a straight wooden axe. Then about thirty years later, in the 1980s, I soloed up this same line in nice névé snow conditions in just a couple of hours, but using two up-to-date axes and equipment, of course, and carrying no more than a water bottle and space blanket. And then another thirty years later, there we are, skiing the thing in spring snow. I guess that's a measure of the way that alpine mountaineering has changed and progressed over sixty years, together with understanding the different conditions.

The Pas De Chevre off-piste ski run that goes down under the north face of the Aiguille du Dru normally takes about half a day to descend the 2,500 metres of vertical down into Chamonix, but early one morning last winter we were lucky and snatched it in perfect, untracked powder snow all the way down, and flew down it in not much more than an hour, almost straight-lining it. At the bottom, a good friend said, 'Hey! This turning lark is all a bit overrated!'

I recently saw a picture in an Alpine climbing magazine, taken from the air above the Chamonix mountains and looking to the south. It showed the north side of the Grandes Jorasses in the background with Mont Dolent, Aiguille de Triolet, Les Courtes and Aiguille Verte in the middle. Then in the foreground it showed the north sides of the aiguilles d'Argentière and du Chardonnet. It felt like my backyard and gave me a huge feeling of pride and contentment to look at this picture and to consider the routes on it that I had done. I'd done one north face on it as a teenager in the 1950s; I'd done one first ascent on the Courtes. I'd done one first British ascent. I'd soloed two of the north faces, the Argentière and the Chardonnet. I'd skied a route off the summit of three of them and guided clients on four of them. 'Inner contentment' is a very special and privileged feeling to be allowed.

As a young kid I'd scrambled up cracks and corners in a local sandstone quarry, in the cheap Woolworths plimsolls that we kids seemed to wear all the time. There were little sandstone or limestone quarries all over County Durham in those days – mind you, they were all overshadowed by the huge, black pit heaps that dominated every pit village then. I'd always been frightened of jumping three metres out of my bedroom window into the back garden, but I was never afraid of being six metres above the ground in those old quarries, as long as I had a little foothold or could reach a bit of a handhold. As a teenager, I played cricket for county schools as a bowler, and second-row rugby for school and then university, and I even rowed a bit. My natural environment as a youth, however, was really riding a rickety old bike over the Pennines, jogging over the moors, messing about in the snow in north-east winters and dossing in makeshift shelters in the woods. I think it's in the genes; I've always been comfortable putting up with cold mountain bivouacs.

I've been fortunate enough to lead 6a rock climbs and grade VI ice climbs, and I've soloed rock climbs, ice climbs and Alpine north faces close to my personal limit. But I think my best habitat was probably pottering up mixed alpine rock and ice climbs with crampons and two ice axes; and nowadays I quite like more of the same, but preferably now with skis strapped to my rucksack for the descents, instead of those knee-crunching ones on foot.

I've skied breakable crust, and even bottomless crust, with a big sack for nearly sixty-five years, and my knees are shot. A few climbing and skiing friends now have two artificial hips and two tin knees, and many are still younger than me, so I consider myself very lucky. After all that skiing 'crud' and 'porridge' and scree descents, I think I'm due a few spare parts soon.

We're all just a product of our accumulated injuries. Many years ago, a rather mature mountaineering client from Denver, Colorado said to me, 'If you're over fifty and get out of bed on a morning without aches and pains, then you must be dead.' I don't know what his theories were for the over-seventies. Trouble is, I was much older than he was even then. Now in my mid-seventies, I'm all aches and pains most of the time, and my knees make clicking noises when I try to bend them.

We're just off out now to have a go at a rock climb that I first did nearly sixty years ago. With a bit of luck and some of my old-age experience we might be all right. 'Old age and treachery is better than youthful enthusiasm.' We'll have to keep a positive attitude because if you think you might fail, then 'sure as eggs', you will fail. Let's hope we get back down to the valley with yet another day survived in the mountains …

… Well, that went okay! There were three of us, and over a cup of tea we worked out that we have a joint age of 237. Now, I don't even drive briskly any more. I just pootle about a bit in my Maserati – just like the old man that I am, I suppose.

Peter's original line drawing for the frontispiece of his handwritten manuscript.
© Peter Allison

Chapter 12
THE FINAL CHAPTER: 'THE BIG C'

This (originally) being chapter number thirteen doesn't bother me one little bit, because I've never been particularly superstitious. I tend to think that you make your own luck a bit. Mind you, getting 'The Big C' isn't exactly good luck – so what do I know? You've just got to get on and face up to whatever life throws at you.

This chapter is not going to be easy – there will be lots of serious, emotional stuff here. In the last two months I've been through spells of intense pain, trying to stabilise my drug treatment, and I've faced terrible feelings about mortality after a lifetime as a climber: I'm in the middle of an emotional rollercoaster.

There has never even been the slightest hint of cancer in my life; it doesn't run in my family. The funny thing is that, some time back, a good ski pal had apparently joked with our other mates that if I kept on soloing up over big alpine bergschrunds and being out in front skiing that untracked stuff, then they reckoned it was definitely one of 'The Big Cs' that would eventually get me: a crevasse! I never dreamt that I was due for a nasty type of cancer – an unwanted, big, fat, inoperable pancreatic tumour that came from nowhere.

How do you go from climbing and skiing in Chamonix to being tied to tubes in an intensive care unit, and feeling as though you're going to die in just a few weeks, without having had some kind of accident? The answer: a sudden, devastating, life-changing illness. It started with a bit of unintentional weight loss, then increasing levels of intense pain, followed by lots of tests and scans.

Initially, we had had a great classic Chamonix powder day: twelve inches of untouched snow, blue skies, big views, rolling terrains, a great group of close friends and lots of laughter – just brilliant. However, I felt more tired than usual – even after easier routes, I was knackered. Only then did I start to accept that the last two weeks of increasing abdominal pain and reduced physical and mental performance were significant. Until you accept that there's a problem, and start to understand the problem, you cannot hope to find a solution. So I took the advice of my nearest and dearest and went to the doctor's.

Within the next three weeks, at five different medical institutions in France, I received the most thorough medical examinations ever, with ECGs and all the bells and whistles: blood tests, endoscopies, MRIs. By then the pain was becoming intolerable. I personally believe in numbers: they're more precise than adjectives. I've always thought that 'a fair bit' or 'it's killing me' is variable for different people; but 0/10 is no pain, and at 10/10 you're dead. So I had crept up from no pain to 8/10.

Then it was diagnosed – an active, four-centimetre-diameter tumour on the serious bit of the pancreas. That's a golf ball sphere that shouldn't be there, spewing out toxic gunge that shouldn't be there. Surgery wouldn't fix it – too near to a big artery and other crucial bits. Radiotherapy wouldn't work on this particular type either. Pancreatic cancer just happens to be one of the most painful types. And I can confirm that. So it's chemotherapy or nothing.

Treatment. Alternatives. France, Lyon, at great expense. Very difficult to travel. It's a no-brainer. Heavy painkillers. Scan pictures and translation of French results into English and a referral through home in North Wales to Liverpool Abdominal Cancer Unit. During the next two weeks, I received all the same slick tests and scans that confirmed the same diagnosis. Plus X-rays showed blood clots spreading into my lungs.

The medical experts must have then considered that I was of a suitable physique, age and previous fitness to opt in to a special trial treatment to test modifications of some of their chemo drugs, and so I signed up as a guinea pig for a bit of experimentation. Half the patients would be given the existing drug treatment and half would be given the new modified drug. I reckoned the monitoring and control of the new drug would be especially good, so I was up for that. I also checked that there was no 'control' section where one third of the group is given nothing at all. I definitely didn't want to be in a group like that.

I'm trying to work towards comparing the feelings and emotions of being 'very poorly' after, say, a climbing accident, where you know you might finish up injured, and those where it's completely shocking and unexpected. Some climbers push the limits so far that they must know that there will be trouble. I've never gone anywhere near that limit, and I haven't 'done' the emotional stuff, either. When you are hit out of the blue with intense pain, and shock and a fear of not surviving, it's extremely emotional and debilitating. There are always ups and downs in life, but I've recently had much worse downs and fears with this illness than I ever had in the mountains when in danger. I confess to a day when I spent several hours curled up in a ball, crying with pain and worry.

A strong side effect of morphine, in a cocktail with other strong pain-killers, together with this particular illness, is constipation – a wonderful after-dinner topic of conversation for middle-class families. I'm now an expert. It can go to various degrees, the ultimate of which is six metres of bowel intestines packed solid – when there's nowhere for the tiniest bit of food, or even tablets, to go to get out of the stomach. There are also no digestive enzymes coming from the pancreas – so nothing gets digested or absorbed.

I was not able to eat anything for the next three weeks, and I lost nearly four stone in weight. If or when you eventually manage to dislodge the build-up, with liberal dosages of something like concentrated Mr Muscle drain cleaner from all ends, it's not a pretty experience.

During one spell in hospital, being hooked up to a drip, my drug injection accidentally went down – there was a burst pipe or something. After about four hours, I started to feel funny. Funny as in 'agony'. If it takes a month for pain to build up from 0/10 to 8/10, the body seems to have the ability to slowly adapt, and almost cope with it. But if pain goes from a controlled ache of 1/10 right up to an unbearable 9/10 in just a couple of hours … it's grim.

I'll be turning full circle in a minute and writing a dissertation about 'Pain and Emotions'. It finally gets us on to a comparison between intensive-care pain and anxiety in hospital, and intense worry and maybe anxiety in a mountain storm, with an exhausted body and the final crux pitch still to go. The difference is, if you make it up the mountain there might not be a charming nurse in white overalls with a syringe and needle to greet you!

During this time of illness, it's nice to have climbing memories to fall back on. I think it's fair to say that during the 1950s, 1960s and 1970s we were doing some pretty challenging British rock climbs, British winter climbs, and technical alpine routes, but I think of my career as mostly being an alpine mountaineer …

Peter Allison passed away in St David's Hospice, Llandudno, on Monday 2 October 2017, aged seventy-five years.

ABOUT THE AUTHOR

Peter Allison studied civil engineering at Nottingham University in the early 1960s and worked for a company of consulting engineers before leaving to develop the family quarrying business with his two brothers. Even though Peter enjoyed inventing practical solutions to engineering problems, his real passion was rock climbing. He started out on Crag Lough in Northumberland as a fifteen-year-old climbing in plimsolls. He moved on to the crags of the Lake District and North Wales, ascending the hardest climbs in those areas at the time. For many years, he continued rock and alpine climbing – including such routes as the *Walker Spur* and the North Face of the Eiger – in parallel with his business career. However, he increasingly found that there was not enough time to realise his mountaineering ambitions, so in the mid-1980s he left the family business and trained to become a mountain guide. From that point, Peter was in his element fulfilling his own aspirations and those of his clients.